P9-DFT-295

ALASKAN APOSTLE

The Life Story of SHELDON JACKSON

J. ARTHUR LAZELL

ALASKAN APOSTLE

The Life Story of SHELDON JACKSON

HARPER & BROTHERS, PUBLISHERS
New York

ALASKAN APOSTLE

Printed in the United States of America

D-K

Grateful acknowledgment is made to the following for permission to reprint selections from the books listed below: The Caxton Printers, Ltd.: *The Eskimo and His Reindeer* by Clarence L. Andrews, copyright 1939 by The Caxton Printers, Ltd.; The Arthur H. Clark Company: *A History of Alaska* by Jeannette Paddock Nichols, copyright 1924 by Jeannette Paddock Nichols; Random House, Inc.: *The State of Alaska* by Ernest Gruening, coypright © 1954 by Ernest Gruening; Charles Scribner's Sons: *Handbook of Alaska* by Maj. Gen. A. W. Greely, copyright 1909 by Charles Scribner's Sons.

Library of Congress catalog card number: 60-8139

CONTENTS

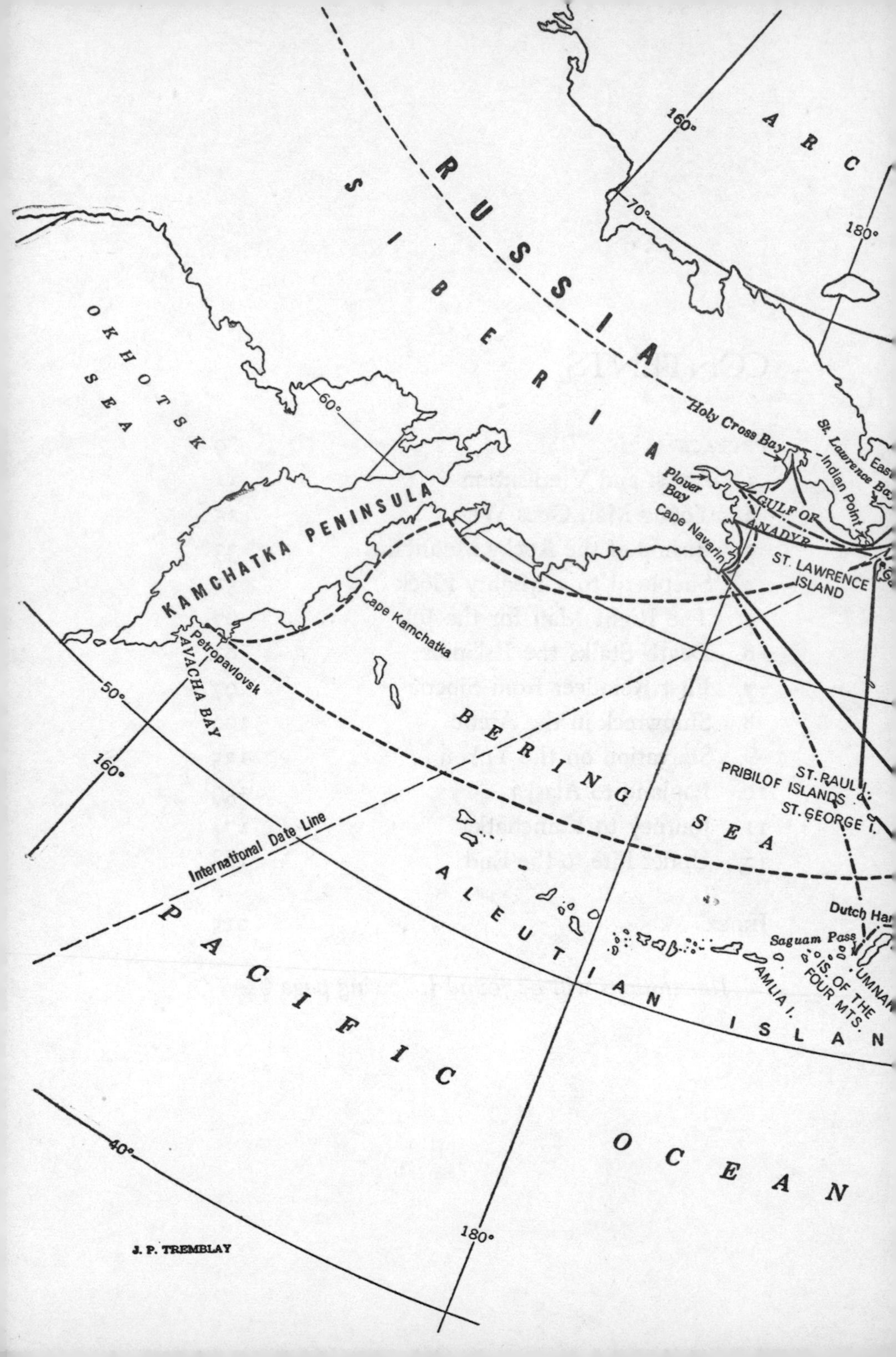

RUSSIA
SIBERIA
OKHOTSK SEA
KAMCHATKA PENINSULA
Petropavlovsk
AVACHA BAY
Cape Kamchatka
Holy Cross Bay
St. Lawrence Bay
Indian Point
Plover Bay
Cape Navarin
GULF OF ANADYR
ST. LAWRENCE ISLAND
BERING SEA
ST. PAUL I.
PRIBILOF ISLANDS
ST. GEORGE I.
International Date Line
ALEUTIAN ISLAN
Dutch Har
Saguam Pass
AMLIA I.
IS. OF THE FOUR MTS.
UMNAK
PACIFIC OCEAN
ARC
160°
70°
180°
60°
50°
160°
40°
180°
J. P. TREMBLAY

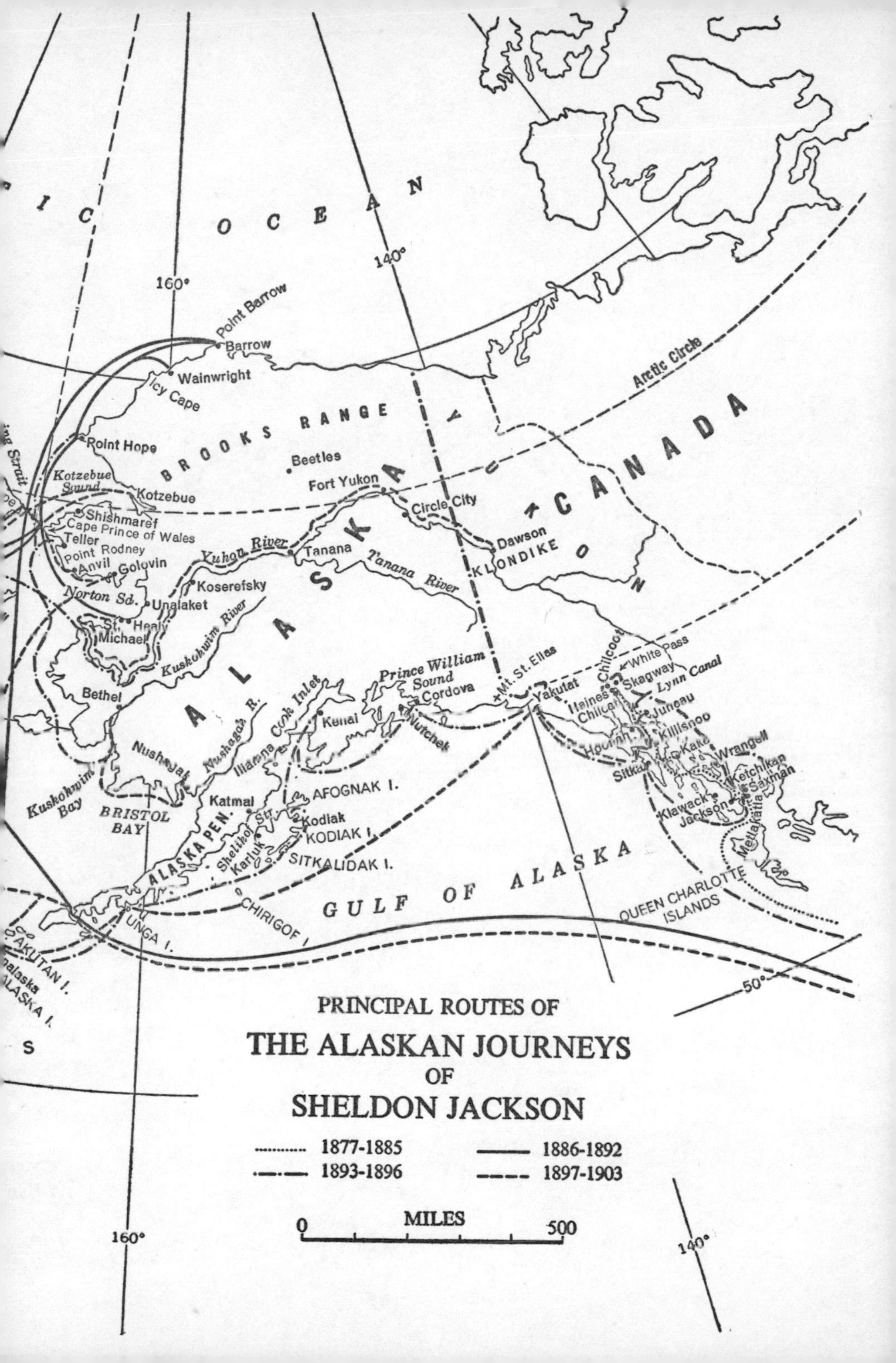

PRINCIPAL ROUTES OF
THE ALASKAN JOURNEYS
OF
SHELDON JACKSON
1877-1885
1886-1892
1893-1896
1897-1903
MILES
0
500
O C E A N
160°
140°
Point Barrow
Barrow
Wainwright
Icy Cape
BROOKS RANGE
Point Hope
Beetles
Kotzebue Sound
Kotzebue
Fort Yukon
Circle City
Shishmaref
Cape Prince of Wales
Teller
Point Rodney
Anvil
Golovin
Yukon River
Tanana
Tanana River
Dawson
KLONDIKE
Koserefsky
Norton Sd.
Unalaket
St. Michael
Healy
Kuskokwim River
Bethel
ALASKA
YUKON
CANADA
Arctic Circle
Prince William Sound
Cordova
Mt. St. Elias
Yakutat
Chilcoot
White Pass
Skagway
Lynn Canal
Haines
Chilcat
Juneau
Killisnoo
Hoonah
Kake
Sitka
Wrangell
Ketchikan
Saxman
Klawack
Jackson
Metlakatla
Kenai
Nutchek
Cook Inlet
Iliamna
Nushagak R.
Nushagak
Kuskokwim Bay
BRISTOL BAY
Katmai
AFOGNAK I.
Kodiak
KODIAK I.
Shelikof Str.
Karluk
SITKALIDAK I.
ALASKA PEN.
CHIRIGOF I.
UNGA I.
AKUTAN I.
GULF OF ALASKA
QUEEN CHARLOTTE ISLANDS
50°

PREFACE

Sheldon Jackson is one of the most exciting and courageous men of all those who worked on the American frontier. The roles he played in Alaska and in the American West form an incredible chapter in the effort of the Church to keep pace with the developing nation.

Jackson was man and missionary, government official and spiritual empire builder. He was responsible for saving the Alaskan Eskimos from extinction and for the founding of Alaska's school system. He did more than any other person in the nineteenth century to inform the American nation about Alaska's needs and people. His failure to accomplish all he hoped to do is, in large part, due to the disgraceful inaction of successive Congresses.

Jackson was prepared to lay down his life as an apostle to Alaska, convinced that "if God be for us, who can be against us?" His spiritual life and moral and physical courage are what churchmen need today if they hope to discharge their responsibilities to the total life of the nation.

Dr. Charles A. Anderson, retired head of the Department of History of the United Presbyterian Church, U.S.A., first turned my attention to Jackson and gave me permission to work on the Sheldon Jackson Collection of the Presbyterian

Historical Society. I appreciate the assistance of members of the Society's staff and the help I received from persons in the Board of National Missions of the United Presbyterian Church, U.S.A. The work of Robert L. Stewart, friend of Jackson and his early biographer, was helpful.

I am grateful to several members of the editorial staff of Harper & Brothers for valuable guidance in writing this book. And there are others closer to me who provided much encouragement.

J. A. L.

CHAPTER 1

ARREST AND VINDICATION

The *Ancon* strained against the two lines still holding her fast to the dock while the crew stood waiting for the signal to shove the gangplank away from her side. Departure of the side-wheel steamer was being delayed by the late arrival of her last passenger, the United States agent for education in Alaska, Sheldon Jackson. Echoing back across the harbor of Sitka from the mountains behind the town, three sharp blasts from the ship's whistle added to the anxiety of the passengers as they stood at the railing. They were friends of Jackson, and they knew how important it was to him that he sail on that ship. He was under orders from the United States Bureau of Education in Washington to open several government schools in southeast Alaska in time for the start of the September term. It was then the middle of August 1885, and Jackson would have to wait another month before the next steamer sailed from Sitka if the *Ancon* left without him. Another long blast from the whistle warned that the captain's patience was at an end and that he was going to leave with or without Jackson. At that moment Jackson's friends caught sight of him about fifty yards from the dock. He was running hard, holding his black derby in place with one hand while his frock coat flapped about him like two black wings. In the distance he appeared even smaller than his meager five feet four inches, and as he pushed his way through the crowd that had gathered to watch the *Ancon* sail, it seemed as if he would never get to the ship. At the foot of the gangplank he paused to catch his breath and, looking about the dock, waved to people he knew. Then he hurried on board. So many of the passengers surrounded him with greetings and expressions of relief that he had to ask several to stand back so as not to interfere with the work of the crew who were putting the gangplank ashore. Just then a deputy United States marshal appeared at the ship's side and called to the captain that he was coming on board. What happened in the next few minutes was the climax to a bitter struggle which had been going on for months in Sitka between Jackson and several other federal officials in the territory.

The deputy wasted no time. He strode up the gangplank, walked straight to Jackson, and said for all to hear that he had a warrant for his arrest. Several of the passengers were so shocked that they could only stare, first at their friend and then at the deputy. Jackson protested vigorously against the summary manner in which the warrant was being served, but before any of the passengers could say or do anything, the deputy took him by the sleeve and hustled him off the ship. Jackson called to the captain to have his baggage put ashore. Almost as if the captain had known what to expect, a crewman darted down the gangplank behind the two men, dropped the bag on the dock, and scurried back to the ship. While the bewildered, half-angry passengers watched, the gangplank was heaved ashore, the lines were cast off, and the *Ancon* started to pull away from the dock. Jackson and the deputy were still a considerable distance from the old Russian jailhouse when the ship's bow swung away from the wharf and the *Ancon* headed out toward the bay. By that time his friends on the ship were talking excitedly among themselves, but there was nothing they could do to aid him. Even if they had been able to remain in Sitka, none of them could have helped. For this last-minute arrest was a prearranged maneuver, part of a plan to discredit Jackson and bring about his dismissal from office.

At that time Jackson was under two thousand dollars bail, awaiting trial on the trumped-up charge that he had built a school in Sitka on property to which he had no rights. Without his knowledge the bail had been increased to thirty-two hundred dollars, and the warrant for his arrest had been issued on the pretext that the authorities in Sitka wanted to make certain he would post the additional bond.

The federal officials involved in the scheme against him were the four top government officers in Alaska, led by E. W. Haskett, the United States attorney. Federal Judge Ward McAllister, Jr., Governor John H. Kinkead, and United States Marshal M. C. Hillyer were the others. These four were appointed by President Chester Arthur in 1884 after Congress passed the first civil code for the District of Alaska, as it was then known, Alaska not becoming a Territory until 1912. Appointing men to office more because of their political sponsorship than for their ability was a practice that plagued American government then as well as now; consequently, none of the four possessed any peculiar qualifications for the positions, though Kinkead had been postmaster in Sitka for a time after the purchase of Alaska in 1867 and had served as Governor of Nevada from 1879 to 1883. But whether they lacked the ability or the desire to be good officials, one point must be made in their defense. Faced with administering a code that was poorly adapted to Alaska's needs, and having little or no means of enforcing the law, it is doubtful whether they or the most highly qualified and dedicated public servants could have discharged the duties of their offices with much success.

Jackson, however, saw only their lapses, and having "little sympathy for fellow Christians who left the narrow way" and understanding "no law beyond that of his conscience," he was not inclined to seek excuses for others. Deeply disturbed by the low moral status of the Indians, for which he felt the white man was largely responsible, and determined to improve their situation, he became the leader of those who opposed Alaska's first officials (as well as their successors) for not giving high enough priority to the needs of the Indians. He made it his business to work toward the removal of Haskett, Kinkead, McAllister, and Hillyer.

This was the general state of affairs which resulted in Jackson's arrest and jailing. But the day-to-day events leading up to the arrest covered a long span of years, starting with the day in 1877 when Jackson came to Alaska for the first time. As a Presbyterian missionary, he came for the purpose of establishing a mission school among the Indians in the territory. During the seven years following the establishment of the school he organized other mission work, recruited missionaries and teachers for the territory, and carried on a one-man campaign in the States on behalf of Alaska and its native population. During those same seven years he made about nine hundred speeches before church groups and secular organizations, enlisted the interest of the National Education Association in developing a public school system in Alaska, and wrote a book about the territory. He acquired the reputation of being an authority on Alaska's needs and problems and in that capacity appeared before a number of Congressional committees in support of legislation designed to give the territory its first civil rule. It was due principally to Jackson's efforts that Congress set up a civil government for Alaska in 1884. Ironically, it was this same law that created the positions held by Haskett, McAllister, Kinkead, and Hillyer.

Ernest Gruening, onetime governor of Alaska and now United States Senator from the forty-ninth state, was speaking of Jackson when he wrote that "however great the handicaps [in Alaska], they were to be vigorously attacked . . . by one who brought to his gigantic task an apostolic fervor which never permitted difficulties to dampen his ardor or diminish his determination."

There were, in fact, several great handicaps to Jackson in his work as agent for education in Alaska. One was the very nature of the possession, for Alaska was a wild, untamed area on which civilization had made very little impression. The few settlements that were scattered along its coastline had little or no effect upon the vast interior but were themselves strongly influenced by the wilderness. Sitka, the largest old settlement in Alaska and the seat of federal authority, was hardly more than a frontier settlement in 1885, with about one hundred and sixty white residents and a thousand Indians, most of whom were half-civilized. The town had one main street, which began at the dock where the *Ancon* had been moored. It "has a beautiful island-studded bay," Jackson wrote. "Mount Edgecumbe, an extinct volcano, guards the entrance to the bay, while the sharp, snowy summit of [Verstovia] surrounded by a group of peaks and glaciers stands guard in the rear." The Russian Orthodox church dominated the village. "Far out beyond the harbor," reads another description, "and as far down the coast as the eye can reach, we have all the variety of grand mountain scenery." A massive and magnificent land, Alaska was largely unknown to the outside world during Jackson's early years there.

Other obstacles with which Jackson had to cope were man-made: lawlessness and immorality, both of which had one root in the nature of man and another in the lack of means of enforcing the law. Out of the latter grew an apathy and a cynicism toward crime and punishment. One of the passengers who had been on board the *Ancon* and had witnessed the arrest prepared a report at the request of a government official who wanted information on the background to Jackson's difficulties. The report pointed out the nature of the man-made obstacle which he faced in Sitka.

". . . ex-governor and ex-United States Senator Booth, of California, was [also] on the excursion and saw the arrest. No one spoke more scathingly of the incompetence of these officials [who] were there for very greedy and selfish purposes. The more disgusting and immoral a town like Sitka could be made, the less opposition would they meet in carrying out their schemes of greed. . . . They did not want the moral power of the missions and schools at the centers where [their schemes] were being carried out. This, I believe, is the key to all the opposition to Dr. Jackson and the Sitka schools."

The industrial training school for native boys, which Jackson had helped to establish, was the particular target of the Haskett group. As the *Ancon's* passenger pointed out in his analysis of conditions in Sitka, the training home was a symbol of authority among the natives which Haskett wanted to destroy. In his efforts to find a suitable weapon, the United States attorney forged a two-edged sword, one side of which he wielded against the home and the other against Jackson.

The side of the weapon to be used against the school was honed to razor-sharpness on the antagonism of some Indian parents. Native children were accepted by the school with the understanding that they were to remain there for five years; it took that long for the youngsters to become accustomed to a new way of life and to learn homemaking and mechanical skills that were unknown to them or their parents. Over the course of a few years, some Indian parents had opportunities to sell their girl children into slavery after the children had been enrolled in the school. The sale of youngsters was a common practice among the Indians for, within their social organization, slavery was an accepted institution which was built around a slave caste. Not only did slavery violate the Christian concept of the worth of the individual, it was also a violation of the Constitution. Court action was taken in Sitka with Haskett's support to demonstrate to the Indians that slavery was illegal and had to be discontinued. But neither moral persuasion nor legal action was sufficient to end overnight so deeply rooted a custom. And, as has been pointed out, the school's insistence on keeping youngsters once they were enrolled, appeared to the Indians to be not different in its restraining effects from the slavery which they had been taught to abandon. Every time a parent sought a child's release—and not always to sell it into slavery—the school authorities were adamant. While most parents were prepared to accept the decision of the school as final, largely because they had no alternative, some were openly resentful. Haskett believed that there was a sufficiently favorable climate in that resentment to gain support among the Indians for his plan to force the school to release one of its students. Once the home was made to break its own rule, the way would be open to getting the release of other pupils. Haskett found out about a half-breed girl who had been placed in the school by her native mother a short time before the mother died. The father had disappeared, leaving no one to contest Haskett's scheme: to bring a half-breed woman from British Columbia to Sitka and have her, posing as a relative of the student, demand the girl's release. The woman reached Sitka early one evening and placed her petition before Judge McAllister at the unusual time of 8:00 P.M. The judge, acting on her request for the girl's release without even bothering to give the impression that he had examined the woman's claim, ordered the home to produce the girl in court that same night. School officials had no alternative but to comply with the court's order. But when they asked McAllister for time to prepare a defense, the judge refused and placed the girl in the woman's custody. The two were on board the steamer when it sailed from Sitka the next morning, convincing school authorities that McAllister and Haskett had planned the whole episode as a means of destroying their work among the Indians.

The judge and the United States attorney had worked out one more phase of the attack upon the school. There was an Indian sorcerer living in the Sitka area who had placed his daughter in the home and subsequently sought her release when he had an opportunity to sell her. The sorcerer offered a ten-dollar bribe to the superintendent of the home for the child's release. When that failed, he proposed that the school accept his son in place of his daughter. As a last resort he even tried to kidnap the girl, but the Indians he hired to do the kidnaping were caught hiding in the forest behind the school and confessed the plot. But now that the half-breed woman had left Sitka with the first student released from the home by court order, the sorcerer was advised to take his complaint before the judge. The result was the same. The girl was ordered released. This time, however, McAllister went a step further and ruled that the school could not make agreements with natives, either written or verbal, thereby wrecking the basis upon which students were accepted. McAllister also warned that he would fine or imprison anyone who interfered with a student's leaving the school. It was not long before one half of the one hundred and four boys and girls in the school had run away, and the influence of the institution among the Indians was reduced to nothing. Thus Haskett had accomplished his objective of ridding himself of the school's authority with the natives. All that remained in his way was Jackson, against whom he prepared the other side of his weapon.

The Presbyterian mission school in Sitka had been moved

from its original site to a 650-acre plot, according to the terms of the school section of the 1884 law. Jackson says that he selected land outside Sitka "beyond all existing fences and improvements on ground that was unclaimed and unimproved woods and swamps, ditching the swamp and grading, in order to prepare a sufficient area of land for the school buildings." He also said that he relocated a road that led out from Sitka and crossed the tract he had selected. However, there appears to be a discrepancy between this account (as related by Jackson in a pamphlet of 1886 in which he explained his difficulties in Sitka) and facts recorded elsewhere, particularly with respect to the relocation and identity of the road. Whatever the facts were, it is clear that Jackson obstructed public passage along a road that led to a burial ground known today as the Sitka National Cemetery. There was apparently not much concern over the school's location or the road obstruction until, as one account reports, a funeral procession headed for the cemetery and found its way blocked by a locked gate. It is said that indignation in Sitka was so high as a result of this incident that Jackson needed the intervention of the civil officials to escape bodily harm. But, at the same time, it appears that Haskett used this antipathy as a means of venting his and the other officials' dislike of Jackson and his methods.

The indictment of Jackson by an 1885 Sitka grand jury impaneled by Judge McAllister charged that he did "unlawfully, illegally, willfully and maliciously, and with malice obstruct a certain road commencing at the beach and in the Town of Sitka and extending to the Public Graveyard and Indian River by erecting thereon a picket fence. . . ." One of the true bills identified the obstruction as "a wagon shed or building."

Later, when Jackson wrote to the foreman of the jury and asked permission to testify in his own behalf, he was further charged with trying to influence the foreman. The judge set

Jackson's bail at two thousand dollars and ordered him to stand trial in Wrangell, which was two hundred miles from Sitka, during the latter part of the summer of 1885. Jackson asked for a postponement of the trial on the ground that the time set for it would interfere with the opening of new government schools. He also asked that the trial be held in Sitka because all of his witnesses lived and worked there and would be forced to make a long and hazardous sea journey in order to testify in Wrangell, in addition to being away from their jobs. McAllister announced on August 17 that he would rule on Jackson's petition for a postponement and change of venue in the very near future. Two days later, on the nineteenth, the judge signed the warrant for Jackson's arrest, and he was removed from the *Ancon* the same day.

But Jackson had not been idle while Haskett was working to destroy the Sitka training school and to besmirch his good name and reputation. Almost from the first day that the Haskett group arrived in Sitka in 1884, he had been gathering information about law violations in the territory and evidence of the failure of the new federal officers to enforce the law. He also compiled a long list of their acts in Sitka and conducted an investigation into their past activities in the States. This information he used to indict the four for incompetency, suggesting but not proving that corruption was a motivating factor. To the Attorney General of the United States he reported that at least thirty saloons were selling liquor openly to the natives, although Congress had prohibited the importation, manufacture, and sale of whiskey in the territory. Dance houses of the worst sort operated illegally, and native girls in their early teens were frequently outraged and sold into prostitution. He also wrote to a fellow missionary, a brother to President Grover Cleveland, that Kinkead was "a broken-down politician . . . of no intellectual or executive force . . . smooth in his words . . . treacherous behind your back. He has spent only two out of eleven months of his term upon his field. . . . At heart he is hostile to the school work." In the same letter he described Hillyer as a gambler, although "a fair man as politicians go."

One of Jackson's sources provided him with an opinion of McAllister: "destitute of almost every attribute which would entitle him to the supreme control of the judicial, legal, and executive offices of a great, half-civilized territory." Former United States Senator Booth, of California, condemned McAllister as being completely unfit for his position as judge "by moral character, habits of life, and lack of knowledge to discharge his duties."

Jackson wrote to President Cleveland that Haskett was "uneducated, rowdyish in his manner, vulgar and obscene in his conversation, low in tastes, spending much of his time in saloons, a gambler and confirmed drunkard, with but little knowledge of the law."

It took time to gather this information, and after it was sent to Washington, more time was consumed while reports went through official channels. As a result, Haskett was able to act against the school and to secure Jackson's indictment before President Cleveland replaced him and the judge, governor, and marshal. Ironically, at the very moment that Jackson was being taken from the *Ancon*, the new officers were on their way to Alaska.

Jackson spent a week in Sitka after being released in higher bail. He then decided to go by canoe to Killisnoo, above Sitka, in the hope of finding a vessel that would take him to the settlements in southeast Alaska where he wanted to open new schools. Finding no other means of transportation at Killisnoo, he continued his trip to Juneau and Wrangell by canoe. In the middle of September he wrote to his wife that he did not see how he could be back in the States before December because of the delays that had been put in his path. "This is very, very hard," he wrote her, "but the Lord has some purpose in it."

While he was away from Sitka organizing the new schools, the second set of officials arrived in the territorial capital. The judge who replaced McAllister made consideration of the indictments against Jackson his first order of business. He ruled that the facts that were supposed to constitute the offenses charged against Jackson would not warrant a conviction and that the charge of obstructing a road, since it was not a criminal act, should have been heard before a justice of the peace. The ruling made by the new judge was a victory and a vindication of Jackson, but unfortunately it came too late to erase the memory of what had taken place. The charges included in the indictment hung over him through all the years that he worked in Alaska. Haskett is reported to have said after his removal from office that his treatment of Jackson was the "worst part" of what he had done in the territory, but this confession was too little and also late. One good result of the dismissal of the indictments and the replacement of the Haskett faction was that the Sitka training school regained its influence with the natives and continued to do excellent work among them for years to come.

There was a third major obstacle to Jackson's efforts in Alaska, an obstacle that blocked the path of all who worked on behalf of the territory. It was the refusal of Congress to pass the laws and to make the appropriations needed to enforce the laws so that Alaska could develop properly. Not only did missions and schools suffer from the failure of successive Congresses to meet the needs of the territory; the entire social and economic development of Alaska was retarded. Jeannette Paddock Nichols in her analysis of the ills that plagued Alaska during its first fifty years under American rule describes Jackson's personal efforts to overcome Congress' sins of omission. She calls him an "ardent apostle of the Presbyterian Church in the mission and educational fields, who occupied a large place in Alaskan affairs at Washington. . . . it is undoubtedly true that the influence of the Presbyterian Church, as exerted by Dr. Jackson acted upon Congress as a powerful lever to overcome its inertia. . . ."

Congressional lethargy and public indifference handicapped every effort to get effective and useful legislation for the district. Many congressmen and government officials felt that Alaska had been foisted on the nation by the ill-advised action of Secretary of State William H. Seward who had encouraged its purchase in 1867 for $7,200,000. Few knew much about Alaska except that it had been owned by Czarist Russia, and much of what they believed was based on half-facts and rumor. The prevailing opinion in and out of government was that Alaska was worthless—a land of towering mountains and massive glaciers, of wild and unnavigable rivers, with a forbidding coastline and an impenetrable interior half-buried under ice and snow, swept by violent winds, and inhabited by heathens. There is the view that Alaska was treated well in comparison with Congress' delay in considering the needs of territories in the American West. But this merely points up the fact that Congress was as lax in aiding the West as it was in helping Alaska. Congress permitted sectional interests, political considerations, and economic pressures to stall action to advance the status of the western territories and Alaska.

There were an estimated 30,000 people living in Alaska in 1867, about two thirds of which were aboriginals—Eskimos, Aleuts, and Indians. The Eskimos still inhabit the northwest and far northern areas of Alaska and were estimated by an 1880-82 census to number 17,617, while an 1885 estimate lowered that figure to 14,012. The Aleuts lived on the Aleutian Islands and the Alaska Peninsula, and were estimated to number 2,145 by the 1880-82 report but 2,950 according to the 1885 figures. The Indians lived in the interior and along the coastal area from Cook Inlet east and in the southeastern section. They were estimated to number 11,478 by the 1880-82 report and 9,519 in 1890. The Russians subjugated the Aleuts but had virtually no contact with the Eskimos and relatively little with the Indians. The combined Eskimo, Aleut, and Indian population in Alaska today is estimated at about 34,000.

Most men would have been overcome by the difficulties Jackson faced in Alaska—the frontier character of the territory, the immorality and lawlessness, the inaction of Congress. Jackson himself would have succumbed to such tremendous odds if he had been nothing more than a well-meaning missionary, intent only on saving the souls of Alaska's native population. But he was a man with a faith, sometimes a little impractical, quite often stubborn, always convinced that one cannot make compromises between the right and the wrong. Political storms and intrigues swept him back and forth. One barrier after another blocked his way. But he persisted in the conviction that he was right, that what he was doing was right. In spite of his shortcomings, he never swerved from his purpose to help the territory and its native people, and Alaska's progress toward statehood cannot be appreciated fully without a knowledge of what Jackson accomplished there.

CHAPTER 2

YOUNG MAN GOES WEST

The years that Jackson worked as a missionary in the American West conditioned him mentally and physically for the exacting life he had to lead in Alaska. From the day that he was rejected for foreign missionary work, through the years he labored in Minnesota, Wisconsin, and the Rocky Mountain region, he learned to face and overcome seemingly impossible odds and to perform feats of daring as if they were everyday occurrences.

He was born on May 18, 1834, in Minaville, upstate New York. His family was known for its strong religious convictions, and his father had the reputation of being a "Presbyterian of the most decided and unwavering type." Jackson made up his mind before he was twenty that he would enter the Christian ministry. He was graduated from Union College in Schenectady and entered Princeton Theological Seminary in the hope that he would be sent to a foreign field. His application was rejected by the foreign board on the ground that he was not strong enough physically, but the board did commission him to teach in its Choctaw Indian mission school at Spencer, Oklahoma. He married Mary Voorhees in May 1858 and six weeks later was at work at the school. A year later he decided that it was not the place for him. He disliked having to whip the boys in order to maintain discipline. Sickness also interfered with his work, and after three attacks of malaria he submitted his resignation.

Next he went to southeastern Minnesota, a sparsely settled region that had been the western tip of the old Northwest Territory. In September 1859 he arrived with an appointment as home missionary to La Crescent and vicinity, for which he was to receive three hundred dollars a year and a house that measured eighteen by twenty-four feet. Assuming that he was to work in as much territory as he could reach, he was soon ministering to an area thirteen thousand miles square. It extended from the town of Jackson in western Minnesota to Chippewa Falls in Wisconsin. Not willing to run the risk of missing anyone, he put up a sign beside the road that led the short distance from La Crescent to the ferry landing on the west bank of the Mississippi River: "Presbyterian immigrants moving west will please leave their names and destinations with the Rev. Sheldon Jackson, so that they may be looked after and church privileges supplied them as early as possible."

Many times in Jackson's career he exhibited a streak of stubbornness. Under some circumstances it served him well, but there were other times when this trait could have had tragic results had it not been that he was destined to live a long and fruitful life. One such occasion, when a greater wisdom than his brought him safely through an experience he could have avoided, took place during the second winter of his work at La Crescent. Having promised to hold an evening church service in a village fourteen miles from his home, he started by sleigh in company with a woman assistant despite the threat of a new storm. It began to snow when they were a few miles from their destination. By the time they were ready to return, conditions were so bad that Jackson agreed to remain in the settlement overnight. It was still snowing the next morning, but he decided to start for home.

It took more than an hour to travel the first mile, with Jackson getting out of the sleigh frequently to lead the weary horse. As the only way to make progress, he walked ahead to break a path for the animal, floundering through the deep snow until he was so exhausted that he had to get back into the sleigh. At one point in the trip the snow was not so deep, and they traveled until late afternoon when the horse stumbled into a snowbank and could not get out of it. Jackson realized that he would have to find a place where he and his companion could spend the night. It was clear that they would not be able to reach La Crescent and that they would die if they remained out in the storm where the wind was increasing and the temperature was falling. The first house Jackson reached was little more than a hut. The man who lived there would have been happy to share his family's small quarters, but Jackson pushed on to the next house—where he was turned away. Returning to the sleigh, he unhitched the horse and on they went, the woman riding while Jackson plodded through the deepening snow. But he fell down so often that soon he too had to mount the horse.

When they reached the hut, they could find no shelter for the animal. Rather than leave it outdoors to die, Jackson decided to go to the house from which he had been turned away, in the hope that the owner would reconsider and give them all shelter for the night. He pounded and shouted until the door opened a crack. Then, putting his face to the opening, he called out that he and the woman were in danger of freezing to death if they could not get indoors. He identified himself as a clergyman, which he had not done the first time he had been there, and that apparently changed the owner's mind. The storm ended during the night, and the following day Jackson and the woman reached La Crescent where they learned that several persons had been lost in the blizzard and had frozen to death.

Even Jackson's persistence was not enough to overcome certain obstacles. There were widespread Indian uprisings in Minnesota during 1862 and 1863 when the Sioux and Dakotas killed about three hundred and fifty persons and captured another two hundred and eighty. The massacres and raids put an end to Jackson's work in the western half of his field while the fear of Indian attacks in the La Crescent neighborhood disrupted his efforts there as well. He was more successful in coping with the impediments of the Civil War upon his work. The economic drain upon the country which resulted from the fighting between the North and the South produced a disastrous reduction in contributions to the mission board and forced a curtailment of all field work. The board had been in financial straits from the time that Jackson started work in Minnesota. Many missionary families less fortunate than his suffered when salary payments were overdue or did not arrive. The lack of funds also hampered the opening of new church work. In spite of the fact that the board tried to discourage him from raising funds from private sources, Jackson believed that he was justified in asking friends and church congregations he knew to contribute to the support of needy missionaries and churches in the La Crescent field. This project was known as the Raven Fund, a name based on the experience of the Old Testament prophet Elijah, who was fed by ravens during a time of drought and famine. The first contribution to the fund was made in December 1860, and subsequent gifts during the next ten years swelled the Raven Fund to almost twenty thousand dollars. Half of this money was spent to build church structures and defray the costs of special church projects, while the remainder went to support needy missionaries. Jackson also asked friends and churches in the East to send boxes of clothing for distribution among his co-workers; these contributions reached him at the rate of more than one a month for ten years.

Jackson once said of himself that if he could not be first, he would try to be foremost. Certainly he ranked foremost in the hearts and minds of the many missionaries who were the beneficiaries of the fund. It was not his most spectacular achievement in a life spent doing the unusual, but it did demonstrate a concern for the needs of others which he maintained throughout his ministry. And it was also evidence of the fact that Sheldon Jackson refused to sit and wait for manna to fall from heaven if he had any way of plucking it from the skies.

The Civil War eventually ended his work at La Crescent largely because he decided that, in the face of the limited opportunity existing there, he could be of greater help elsewhere. Several private groups had been organized to provide Union Army chaplains with assistants. To one of these, the Christian Commission, Jackson applied for work and was sent to Tennessee. He arrived there during the first week of August 1863. The North's Army of the Cumberland had battled its way east across Tennessee and was bottled up in Chattanooga by then. But to the west, at Winchester, there was a Union army camp, a hospital, and a compound for Confederate prisoners-of-war. Jackson was assigned to work at Winchester, visiting the hospital and camp, distributing Christian literature, helping soldiers write home, and giving pastoral help to all who wanted it. He was most surprised to find that large numbers of soldiers attended church services. A month after he reached Winchester, the bloody battle of Chickamauga added thousands of sick, wounded, and dying to the overcrowded town. But Jackson stayed with the work, undaunted by the round-the-clock demands made on him, until he received word of illness in his family at La Crescent. After serving only two months as a

Christian Commission delegate, he returned to Minnesota and became critically ill himself with typhus contracted during the work in Tennessee. It was a long time before he was able to return to his mission post. When he did, he divided his time between the field and the copastorate of the Presbyterian Church in Rochester, Minnesota. Eventually, he became the full-time minister of the congregation. This was the only period when he devoted himself completely to one church, excepting the small congregation at La Crescent. At Rochester as at La Crescent, however, he found additional duties to occupy whatever time weighed upon him. He remained in Rochester until 1869 when the urge to return to missionary work became so strong that he resigned in order to satisfy it. A friend of Jackson once said of him that he could not escape the desire to be "running ahead of the crowd, climbing a hill, scaling a mountain, following a valley, opening a schoolhouse . . . constantly searching out the land." And so it was in 1869, with his desire to search out the regions west of the Mississippi, that he came to grips with the problems that faced the Church on the frontier. He went to Sioux City, Iowa, in April 1869, to attend a presbytery meeting of his fellow ministers and there experienced the spiritual urge that led him to explore the great Rocky Mountain region for the sake of the Church and, at last, to work in Alaska.

On the outskirts of Sioux City, there is a high point overlooking the Missouri River which is known as Prospect Hill. A man standing at the summit can see parts of Iowa, Nebraska, and Dakota. Jackson and two other clergymen, John C. Elliott and Thomas H. Cleland, Jr., walked to the top of that hill to look at the lands that stretched westward so that they might visualize the plains and mountains beyond the horizon where there were people who needed the Church. They talked about the opportunities for the Church in the West and the importance of keeping pace spiritually with the men and women who were on the distant frontiers. They were deeply disturbed by the fact that many who had emigrated to the West had left their churches behind them. The Church, they felt, had to assume the responsibility of going after these people. After talking about what had to be done, the three of them knelt in prayer, asking for the wisdom and strength required to do the work they had in mind. Later, when they spoke to the presbytery about the vision of service they had had on Prospect Hill, their words rang with the passion of men prepared to give all of themselves. So convincingly did they speak that the meeting voted to expand its missionary efforts, and Jackson was appointed missionary superintendent for Iowa, Nebraska, Dakota, Idaho, Montana, Wyoming, and Utah. His was a 571,000 square mile parish.

It was not by chance nor by the Prospect Hill experience alone that Jackson received his new assignment. After deciding to leave the Rochester church and re-enter the mission field, he had asked several Presbyterian regional bodies to appoint him to do missionary work within their bounds. Three presbyteries besides the Sioux City meeting commissioned him to work in the same western areas, but not one of the four groups could pay him a salary. They were even without funds to support the work which they had authorized him to perform. Jackson admitted some years later that some people probably thought him a little foolhardy for having accepted such responsibility without knowing where he would get the money to support himself or his assistants. He handled the problem of raising funds in the same way that he had developed the Raven Fund: by asking friends and church groups to support the work. In the two years that followed his acceptance of this new commission, he raised more than ten thousand dollars for missions to the vast new regions to the west.

When he left Sioux City on the first of May 1869, Jackson was full of plans for the future. Foremost in his mind was the fact that the Central Pacific and Union Pacific Railroads were only a few miles apart in northern Utah. He saw that the linking of the two lines would start a new wave of migration to the West and that it was essential for representatives of the Church to be on hand to provide spiritual services when the settlers arrived. The golden spike that was driven into place at Promontory, Utah, on May 10, 1869, gave to the United States its first transcontinental railroad. An army band was on hand to herald the event. A magnetic ball on top of the Capitol in Washington was dropped at the moment of the joining. Guns boomed out a salute in San Francisco. But there was no fanfare to mark the fact that, several days earlier, Jackson had succeeded in locating three missionaries at points along the transcontinental railroad west of Sioux City. One man was in charge of a 375-mile area extending to Julesburg in northeast Colorado; another had responsibility for the work along a 315-mile stretch that ended at Rawlins in south-central Wyoming; while the third served the 292 miles from Sweetwater Mines and Green River in Wyoming to Corinne, Utah. New workers were added as rapidly as possible during the next twelve months. Great missionary activity was soon spreading in every direction of the compass from these three areas, the long-range results far exceeding the immediate rewards.

But just as it was Jackson's personal drive that set this missionary effort in motion, so it was his capacity for going it alone that brought him into conflict on occasion with his denomination's home mission board. He was responsible to the presbyteries that had given him the authority to work within their bounds, but he also had an obligation to maintain good relations with the board in New York. It is true that poor communications between the West and the East made it difficult for him to establish satisfactory contact with those who had responsibility for the over-all missionary work of the Church. But the heart of the difficulty was that Jackson and the board disagreed over whether or not the work was being expanded too rapidly in the West. New York resolved the question in the light of its perennial lack of funds for new projects, while it was Jackson's inclination to open new fields and then discover means of maintaining them. He was disturbed to think he gave the impression that he was ignoring the board's wishes. He explained his feelings by saying, "I have made this subject a matter of earnest prayer and now feel that 'woe is me if I do not enter upon the work.' While I greatly prefer to work under the [board's] commission, yet, if [it] cannot appoint me, I most earnestly desire that they would consider me just as loyal to them as if working for [them]."

Differences were resolved in part when the board commissioned him as a missionary late in 1869 at fifteen hundred dollars a year with no travel allowance. He felt that the board acted as a result of his success in raising funds and because it recognized that he was doing a good job. At this time he was relieved of responsibility for Iowa, but Colorado and New Mexico were added to his field. Nebraska and Dakota were assigned to other men in 1870. Several years later Arizona also came under Jackson's charge. He moved his family to Council Bluffs in May 1869 so that his home might be closer to his field and then set out on his first trip into the Rocky Mountain area, where he labored for seven years. His first stop on this journey was Cheyenne, which he described as a "city of shanties, only two years old"; but because he considered it a town of "great prospective importance," he organized a congregation there. At this point he had to interrupt the trip in order to raise funds back East. When he was able to resume it, he traveled by Union Pacific to Bryan, Wyoming, there to meet a stagecoach which would carry him the one hundred miles over wasteland to South Pass, Wyoming, on the Continental Divide. Since Indians were reported to be on the warpath, only one other passenger besides Jackson was willing to make the journey. Both men held loaded rifles on their knees in case of attacks while the stage raced the ten- and twelve-mile stretches between fortified stockades. When they reached South Pass late at night, Jackson put up at a hotel where he paid four dollars for a night's sleep in one of three double beds crowded into a room twelve feet square. The following day he found several persons who were interested in starting a Presbyterian church, and after forming the congregation, he conducted the first service in a warehouse located on the edge of town. The remainder of the trip took him to Corinne in Utah, Helena in Montana, Rawlins and Laramie in Wyoming, and Grand Island, Columbia, Blair, and Fremont in Nebraska. During one part of the journey he rode a stage continuously for four days and nights, curling up to sleep on a board seat four and a half feet wide.

He organized congregations at each of the principal points he visited on this trip and solved the problem of finding permanent quarters in which the new congregations could worship. He contracted with a Chicago firm to ship and assemble prefabricated structures on lots purchased by the new congregations. One official of another denomination asked plaintively why his missionaries did not profit from Jackson's example. The answer, of course, was that to emulate Jackson one had to be like him. But how many could be found to follow in the footsteps of a man who, in his first year of work in the Rocky Mountain area, traveled twenty-nine thousand miles and organized twenty-two churches?

CHAPTER 3

BISHOP OF THE ROCKY MOUNTAINS

Utah was one of the Rocky Mountain territories under Jackson's care where nature's barriers were easier to scale than those erected by men. Jackson had his first look at the Great Salt Lake valley about a quarter of a century after Brigham Young settled his Mormon brethren there. Like Young, he felt that the valley was a good place in which to start building for the future. But by the time Jackson arrived on the scene, the Mormon hierarchy so controlled the religious, social, and economic life of the territory that few outside of the Mormons could get anywhere in building a future for themselves. The Mormons wanted to live apart from the "gentiles" and were spurred in their opposition to the missionary work of outsiders when the transcontinental railroad weakened their grip on Utah by ending its isolation.

In spite of Mormon hostility, non-Mormons were attracted to the region in increasing numbers by the prospect of making a good living, and these people provided the nuclei around which several denominations made missionary efforts. The Congregationalists were among the first, but when the superintendent of one of their Sunday Schools was shot, presumably but not provably by Mormons, Congregationalist work languished in Utah. The Episcopalians also made an effort to organize churches but had little or no success. Henry Kendall, the senior secretary of the Presbyterian Board of Home Missions, had been invited to preach in Salt Lake City as early as 1864, but the Presbyterians were no more successful than other denominations until Jackson arrived on the scene.

He started by making a survey of the possibilities of organizing a congregation in Corinne and, with a good report in hand, established a church there in 1870. Unfortunately for the future both of the congregation and of the town, Brigham Young picked Ogden instead of Corinne as the place where his Utah Northern Railroad should join the Union Pacific. Corinne became a way station on a branch line, and the growth of the town and the church was stunted permanently. However, Jackson made every effort to develop the new church. He made 1,300-mile round trips between Corinne and Denver, where he had moved his family in July 1870, so that the Corinne church might have services during a period when it lacked a minister.

In Salt Lake City he organized another church (this one with twelve members), placed a minister in charge of it, and left to the future the problem of its support. For a time the new congregation had to worship in any quarters it could find, including an ice-skating rink. When a campaign to raise money to build a church structure fell short of its goal, the Salt Lake City minister went East to revitalize the drive, Jackson meanwhile handling the preaching and pastoral responsibilities. He used the occasions to explore the opportunities for organizing other churches, one of which he located at Alta, thirty-five miles southeast of Salt Lake City near the famous Emma Mine. Alta was a difficult place in which to work, for as late as June there might be five feet of snow in the center of town. When Jackson went there, he visited homes by walking on planks laid from the top of snowbanks to the second-floor windows. The missionary assigned to work in Alta lived in a room above a combination grocery and whiskey store. He wrapped himself in a feather comforter for protection against stray bullets when brawling miners were settling their differences on the street below his room.

Jackson had a habit of answering requests for advice by offering a challenge—which was how the next Presbyterian church came into being in Utah. The Rev. Duncan McMillan was in poor health and in search of a pastorate in a healthy climate when he met Jackson for the first time. Jackson told him that he ought to try Mount Pleasant, about a hundred miles south of Salt Lake City. McMillan, equal to the spur, assumed his new responsibility with great eagerness, only to discover that the Mormons had no intention of letting him labor in peace. He had been in Mount Pleasant only a short time when he was awakened from sleep one night by the sound of someone trying to break into his bedroom. He lay motionless for a few minutes, not knowing what to do, then picked up a loaded revolver and crouched beside the window to repel the marauder. All was so quiet for a time that he thought he had imagined the disturbance, but then he heard someone raising the sash. The barrel of a revolver appeared in the window and a face rose above the sill. McMillan struck at the figure with the barrel of his gun. There was a cry of pain, the thud of a body hitting the ground, and the sound of feet running into the night. He closed the window without looking out and returned to bed, the revolver beside him.

On other occasions McMillan was the victim of Mormon cold war tactics, as they tried to do by intimidation what direct methods had failed to accomplish. To show to the Mormons that he was determined to remain in Mount Pleasant, he posted a notice in the post office advertising a special church service.

One of the town's residents came to McMillan beforehand to warn him that an attempt would be made on his life if he went ahead with the service. At the appointed hour, he looked out over the audience hoping to recognize his would-be assailants. When he saw the mayor of the town and a Mormon bishop, he invited them to take places on the platform. But the two men declined and McMillan mounted the makeshift pulpit alone. He placed a loaded revolver on the table beside the Bible and started the service. When he announced the hymn and started to sing, his was the only voice raised in praise, for his audience had come more for the purpose of seeing how he would react to the threat than for religious reasons. He read from the Bible, offered prayer, preached a brief sermon, then pocketed his gun and went home without being molested. McMillan remained in Mount Pleasant for five years. Eventually he took charge of the Presbyterian work in Utah when Jackson was concentrating on other areas.

The Mount Pleasant story illustrates Jackson's gift for finding the right men to do the work that had to be done. Furthermore, the men who worked with Jackson felt great loyalty toward him. There were exceptions to this pattern, but for the most part his genius in surrounding himself with dedicated and courageous men was one of the essential ingredients in his success.

Another missionary who was willing to dare physical hardship in the style Jackson seemed to prefer for himself was the Rev. George Darley. Stationed in Colorado, Darley was Jackson's counterpart in daring. His parish was bound by the massive sides of the Uncompahgre Plateau and the San Miguel Mountains, with sky for a ceiling and the rugged terrain for a foundation. With his own hands Darley built the first Presbyterian church on the Pacific side of the Great Divide at Lake City, Colorado, and when Jackson encouraged him to expand his field, he started on a 125-mile trip to the mining community of Ouray in spite of unfavorable weather. With a young companion he set out on a little-used trail through mountain wilderness inhabited solely by a band of Ute Indians who lived at an Indian Agency two thirds of the way to Ouray.

The big obstacle that lay in their path was Engineer's Peak. The two men crossed the eastern slope of the mountain with ease, but they ran into difficulty as soon as they started the ascent of the main spur. Snow lay four feet deep along many stretches of the narrow trail. Huge boulders jutted overhead, while the path skirted canyons hundreds of feet deep where one misstep would be the last. Only on the first night, when they found a deserted miner's cabin, were they able to rest. The second day's traveling was as difficult as the first. Huge icicles hung from the rocks above the trail and the snow remained knee-deep. During the third afternoon when Darley and his companion were on the west side of the peak, a snowstorm struck and raged throughout that day and night on into the fourth day. The storm was followed by a sharp drop in temperature and a rising wind that drove the cold through their clothing and numbed their bodies. Their eyelids became swollen, and in their half-blind state they had to stop every few yards to make certain they had not wandered off the trail. The little burro that packed most of their provisions suffered so much from the bad weather that they had to shove and pull the beast to keep it moving. When at last they were only a few miles from the Indian Agency and were feeling secure for the first time, they found that they still had to cross the flooding Uncompahgre River—twenty times! It was late at night before they finally reached the Agency, their arms and legs bloated and painfully inflamed from wading through the icy water. Darley took only a brief rest even though he was exhausted from lack of sleep and, having had his first hot meal in two days, resumed the trip to Ouray. He was impressed with the need for a church there and so reported to Jackson, who asked Darley to return to Ouray with him in the spring to organize the congregation. When early warm weather began to melt the snow and send torrents of water into the valley, they set out together from Lake City. But stretches of the lower trail were wiped out, and Darley decided that the only way to Ouray was by an upper pass. Jackson vividly tells the story of the hazards they faced:

"We rode up the canyon of Hanson Creek for ten miles, between lofty rock walls from 100 to 1,000 feet high. After a good dinner we shouldered our blankets and provisions and started on foot up the canyon. All along were beautiful waterfalls and cascades a thousand feet high. Here and there we passed where an avalanche had cut a broad swathe down the mountainside, carrying away the trees, both stumps and limbs. Five miles up, at the edge of the snow line, we came to a new log cabin where we camped for the night. About sundown, the clouds began to gather and the snow to fall, and with it fell our hopes of crossing. . . . Soon the clouds floated away and the sky cleared. Our blankets were spread upon a pile of shingles and I was soon sleeping soundly. Mr. Darley, who could not sleep, kept the fire burning and amused himself by throwing chips at the chipmunks that played about the floor and ran over our beds. About 2 A.M. he woke me with the announcement that breakfast was ready. Eating bacon, biscuit and coffee, we were on our way by half-past three to get over the crust before the morning sun should soften it.

"We floundered over the fallen timber in the dark, felt our way over logs across the streams or waded them, and when boots and socks were thoroughly wet, we found a grim satisfaction in wading all subsequent streams rather than balance on an uncertain log. In an hour we were at timber line, or an elevation where timber ceased to grow. We now started zigzag up the vast field of frozen ice and snow. The air grew rarer and rarer, and breathing became more and more difficult. The wet boots became frozen and the wet feet ached as if they were freezing too. Up, and still up, we went. Each step the heel of the boot was driven firmly into the frozen snow—each one trying to step in the dent made by the one ahead of him. A misstep would send the unlucky traveler whirling down the snowface of the mountain, to be dashed to pieces on the rocks below. Every few steps, securing our heels in the snow, we would lie out at full length exhausted, heart thumping, nose bleeding, eyes running, and ears ringing. Sometimes the blood was forced from both eyes and ears.

"From near the summit a rock was sent whirling down the vast snowfield until, a mile below, it seemed like a top spinning on the floor. Daylight was approaching and still we were climbing painfully until, as the first rays of the morning sun were lighting up a hundred grand mountain peaks around, we gained the summit—13,500 feet. What a panorama greeted our eyes! On either side was Mt. Sickels and Engineer's Peak. Off to the north, the great Uncompahgre Peak, 14,235 feet high, was head and shoulders above his fellows. Far away to the west, in the dim blue distance, was the Wasatch Range of Utah. As far as the eye could reach in every direction was a wilderness of peaks, and all covered with snow, with the exception of some rocks too steep for the snow to lie upon. Nothing but snow was visible—a Canadian January scene in the middle of June.

"It was too cold to tarry and we were soon plunging down the western face of the mountain. Where it was not too steep, we ran down the snow, and where it was too steep for running, we would sit and slide. Such a slide of a thousand feet at breakneck speed might well be the great event of the season for the average schoolboy. Between running and sliding we were down in twenty minutes, a distance that on the other side had cost us two hours of painful climbing, and were at the first cabin on the headwaters of the Uncompahgre River. Without halting, we plunged down the canyon, as there was yet considerable snow to be crossed. The descent was rapid, and the trail bordered with a constant succession of waterfalls, anyone of which would have repaid a trip of hundreds of miles. Soon after reaching the timber line the snow ran out, and we had a succession of dry ground, mud, and fording the mountain torrents. Down we went until we reached Poughkeepsie Creek, which runs through a wild and almost inaccessible canyon to join the Uncompahgre from the west. Here we lost the trail and got off into the fallen timber. By the time we found it, my feet were so blistered, traveling in wet and at times frozen boots, that I could go no farther. We were in the heart of the mountains, still ten miles from town.

"It was decided that Mr. Darley should leave the provisions and blankets with me, and push on to Ouray and send back a horse to carry me in. Building a fire and spreading the blankets I went to sleep, with my feet drying at the fire. Four hours passed and [Darley] returned without the horse. Shortly after leaving me, he had again become lost, and, wandering around, found himself at the bottom of a deep canyon. The water of the mountain torrent filled it from rock to rock, shutting off farther progress. To extricate himself from that gorge, he had climbed great pine trees, that like stairs enabled him to get from one ledge of rock to another. On his return, he had met a miner going to Ouray and, being too much exhausted to walk with him, had sent a note informing the Presbyterians of our situation. After a good rest in camp, a burro pack train came along and we hired our passage into Ouray. . . . The trail led up and down mountainsides so steep that, going up, we had difficulty in keeping from sliding off behind and, in going down, we felt like bracing with our feet behind the animal's ears, and along the edge of precipices where the giving away of a stone would send both animal and rider into the foaming river a thousand feet below. Just before reaching the village, we met a party with horses and provisions coming to our relief, and soon after we were safe among friends. The First Presbyterian Church of Ouray was organized on June 13th."

It would have been understandable if Jackson had been discouraged from doing further work in Colorado after his experiences on the trip to Ouray. The state's population was small and scattered, and travel from one isolated community to another was both arduous and uncertain. The mining boom of the late 1870's had brought in thousands of people and transformed tiny settlements into boisterous cities almost overnight. But Jackson was as determined to prospect for spiritual wealth among the newcomers as they were to wrest riches from the earth. He came to the conclusion that Leadville, some one hundred and fifty miles north of Ouray, could be a focal point for work in the north central part of Colorado. In the summer of 1878 he went there with that purpose in mind. Like many other places in the state, Leadville had been a mining village of about two dozen roughhewn cabins and a muddy road before the great silver discoveries. As the treasure poured forth from mines like the Little Pittsburgh and the Matchless, Leadville's single street became many muddy roads, and the cabins turned into a city of ten thousand people. Greed and violence, riches and poverty, hope and despair intermingled as men fought one another and the earth in their craving for wealth. Every other door in Leadville opened into a saloon, a dance hall, or a gambling house when Jackson arrived there. A contemporary description of Sunday in Leadville spoke of God as the "crucified carbonate," which was the unrefined ore from which silver and lead were extracted.

By the end of 1878 the Leadville congregation of thirteen people, organized by Jackson in August, was worshiping in a rough, pine board building with unpainted walls and cheap stained-glass windows. Several years later the congregation numbered two hundred and sixty-four, but as the mines were worked out and Leadville declined in size and importance, the church suffered the fate of the town. The same pattern of rise and fall was characteristic of other churches which Jackson organized in the West and Southwest, and some of them even passed out of existence. As a result, he was criticized for using poor judgment in organizing congregations in such out-of-the-way places. But there was a need for them at the time they were established, and not all the wisdom of contemporary second-guessers can detract from the fact that Jackson took the Church to people who wanted it when they needed it.

Jackson never limited his activities to projects that were popular. For example, many people felt that it was a waste of time and money to do any mission work among the Indians of the Southwest, but Jackson wanted to help Indian children and he allowed nothing to get in the way. He accepted a commission as agent of the Board of Indian Commissioners in Washington for the purpose of gathering a group of Indian children and placing them in the government training schools at Hampton and Carlisle. The assignment seemed routine enough, and Mrs. Jackson, who accompanied her husband occasionally on journeys that did not involve hardships, went along to help with the children. Leaving their two small girls with friends in Denver, the Jacksons went to Albuquerque to take the Santa Fe railway south through New Mexico on the first leg of the trip. They did not know that an Apache uprising had New Mexico in turmoil, particularly around Mesilla and Deming, through which they had to travel to reach several Indian reservations in Arizona.

Passenger service on the Santa Fe ended at San Marcial, and persons bound for Mesilla had to transfer to a construction train for the remainder of the trip. But the Jacksons missed their connection by an hour and had to remain overnight in San Marcial. It was bitterly cold. The wind swept down from the snow-covered Magdalena Mountains making it impossible for them to keep warm even around a red-hot stove inside a temporary canvas hotel. Jackson and his wife spent a restless night on cots in a six-by-eight-foot shanty. Because of the intense cold, the hotelman's clock stopped during the night. They awakened, therefore, with just enough time to catch a southbound work train. After stumbling along a quarter mile of track in the early morning darkness, they boarded an immigrant car filled with the odor of cigar smoke and raw whiskey, the clamor of miners, gamblers, and saloonmen. The trip to the end of the tracks was miserable; they were happy to get off the train and take a stagecoach for Mesilla. Here they boarded another stage for a twenty-mile journey across the desert to the extremity of the Southern Pacific Railroad. Another construction train took them north to Deming to make connection with a passenger train for Tucson. Unfortunately, they missed connections again. But rather than stay overnight in Deming without a place to sleep, they continued north with the work crew, reaching Tucson at four in the morning.

Mrs. Jackson remained in Tucson while her husband went by stage to the Pima and Maricopa Indian Agency to collect the first group of children. Next he stopped at the San Carlos Apache Agency one hundred and twenty miles away; here he had to persuade some of the Indian parents that it was in the best interest of the boys and girls to allow them to attend the government schools. The trip back to Tucson took him through one of the most desolate sections of the Southwest. The road was nonexistent in many places. At one point passengers and driver had to walk while the wheels of the stage were chained and the horses put to the gallop to prevent the coach from overrunning the animals.

Indian attacks were so widespread by the time the Jacksons were prepared to leave Tucson that they were advised to delay starting the return trip. Jackson, however, got the railroad district superintendent to provide a special car that could be barred against intruders and have it coupled to a southbound train. There were no troubles with the Indians during the trip to Deming, but to the east in the region around Mesilla new attacks had been reported. Mesilla was a sprawling, dirty town of about one thousand persons, most of them poverty-stricken farmers and sheep herders of mixed blood. The scalping of a Mexican family and several herders and miners near the town had turned the Mexicans' normal dislike of the Indians into hatred of them and anyone connected with them. Jackson had passed through Mesilla on his way to Tucson, but it had been late at night, and he knew nothing about the town or the people who lived there. Now he was anxious to reach the Santa Fe Railroad and start on the final phase of the trip to Hampton and Carlisle. So in spite of the warnings he received, he telegraphed for a wagon train to meet his party at the end of the Southern Pacific tracks. He also asked for an army detail to provide safe passage through the area around Mesilla. Actually, the real danger came from a source other than the Indians. Word had reached Mesilla that a group of Indian children were on their way east, and a party of Mexicans had ridden out from Mesilla to ambush the youngsters.

It was night when Jackson and his party reached the end of the Southern Pacific. He was met there by a fellow missionary who worked in the Mesilla area. He told them about the trap but added that if they started at once in the wagons he had brought, they could circle above the ambush. It is not clear why Jackson did not wait for the Army escort he had requested; perhaps he had not received a reply to his telegram and thought that the Army could not help. In any event, the missionary assured him that the trip could be made safely, and the sleepy, unsuspecting children were bundled in blankets and put to bed. Shortly after midnight, the wagon train left the railroad construction camp, turned off the trail almost at once, and circled north into the hill country parallel to the trail. It was a rough trip, and the drivers had to depend more on the instinct of the animals than their own knowledge of the country. At daybreak the wagons headed south and rejoined the trail, having passed the waiting Mexicans during the night. Then the Army escort arrived and took the Jackson party around Mesilla to the Santa Fe where the children were put on a train for San Marcial.

Meanwhile, Indian trouble had developed once more. The mutilated bodies of four Mexicans were brought into San Marcial the same afternoon Jackson arrived. He was warned that if the Mexicans found out about the Indian children, everyone in his party would be torn limb from limb. Therefore, when the train had entered the station and the other passengers had gotten off, the Jackson car with everyone in it was backed into the comparative safety of the railroad marshaling yard. It was a stiflingly hot afternoon, but the car doors had to be kept locked and the shades drawn so as to attract as little attention as possible. Jackson and his wife spent three terrifying hours with the children in San Marcial.

Only when they felt the jolt of their car as it was coupled to a northbound passenger train were they able to relax in the knowledge that they had escaped a horrible death.

This was one of the last trips that Jackson made as a missionary to the Rocky Mountain region. The 1870's were drawing to an end, and he was beginning to feel the lure of Alaska. The mission board had acted on his request to be relieved of most of his responsibilities in the West and Southwest, although one assignment which he retained had enabled him to make a peculiarly important contribution to the Church during the years he labored in those states and territories: the editorship of the *Rocky Mountain Presbyterian*. This was a four-page monthly paper which Jackson had founded in 1872. He did some of the editorial work and a good part of the reporting whenever and wherever he found an opportunity: on horseback, in trains and stages, on a rock beside a trail while he waited for a coach. The paper was filled with vivid details and illustrations of the importance of home missions. The shortage of missionaries, the hazards of their work, the financial and spiritual needs of the Church on the frontier were all reported in its pages. Jackson exhorted his readers to contribute money and service to the various projects, advising them of those that were already under way and those that should be started. The *Rocky Mountain Presbyterian*, because it provided such an excellent picture of the people, places, and problems of the West, became a successful forerunner of other promotional publications in the mission field.

Jackson's ability to carry on this editorial responsibility in addition to everything else he did is a tribute to his dedication and tenacity. For in the seven years that followed the Sioux City experience, he traveled more than two hundred and twelve thousand miles, organized sixty-seven Presbyterian congregations and erected thirty-six church buildings. He always regretted the fact that a shortage of ministers prevented the organization of more congregations. When he was asked on one occasion to describe the conditions under which he labored in the Rocky Mountains, he wrote that "if any have ever tried the torture, the living martyrdom, of riding in a stage coach from Monday evening to Sunday morning, day and night, without stopping except for a few minutes at a time to change teams—sometimes with three meals and sometimes with only one in 24 hours—and even that so poor and dirty that only hunger forced eating, then you will have some conception of the amount of physical fatigue and suffering that is crowded into those trips."

He felt that his experiences had involved physical hardships few men could or would have endured. Stage coaches were robbed on five occasions either just before or immediately after he had passed over the route. Once as he started to board a stage along a lonely stretch of road, he found himself staring into the gun barrels of a sheriff's posse. The deputies in the coach, mistaking him for a friend of their prisoner, thought he was attempting to hold up the stage and release the man. By his own admission he was accustomed to going to bed on occasions with a loaded revolver as protection against enemies. His life was threatened by prairie and mountain fires.

Under the matter-of-fact manner in which he detailed his experiences, he sometimes felt that his burdens were too great for one man and that he was being asked to do too much. If this was true, Jackson, in a sense, was responsible for his own predicament, for he found it impossible to say No. On the other hand, whenever he felt that he had had enough, he "pressed forward again, thankful for the privilege of laboring and suffering for Jesus."

Jackson felt that he had learned two lessons during his Rocky Mountain work. He described one as the need for a firmer trust in God; the other, for cultivating what he described as "an aggressive spirit." No one who knew him was surprised when he said that "God blesses aggressiveness. We need to cultivate an aggressive spirit. An asking of God for great things—an expectation of great things from God—and an attempting of great things for God" is the responsibility of every Christian. He believed that he was led to work in the Rocky Mountains, "not for a living—not for health—but as ambassador of the Lord Jesus Christ to do the greatest good to the greatest number."

There were, of course, some lessons that Jackson never learned. Among them was the necessity for keeping his superiors fully informed about what he was doing and where he was working. In this deficiency he was a trial to Kendall, his close friend and superior. Kendall, the top-ranking executive of the home mission board, seldom knew where to reach his field general. Kendall was the strategist and depended on him for information on which to make certain decisions. Kendall was also faced on many occasions with the need for protecting Jackson's work (less so, the man) from shortsighted, carping criticism. In one request for information the board secretary wrote, "Where you are now, what you have been doing since, where your wife and children are, where anybody is by whom we can reach you by letter, I know not, but I strike in the dark." He might have started every letter to Jackson with that paragraph.

Persons who were much nearer to the field than Kendall also had a hard time keeping track of Jackson. The editor of a Colorado Springs newspaper, who dubbed him the "bishop of the Rocky Mountains," said that it was "worth a man's life almost to keep in sight even of [Jackson's] coattails as he glides around the mountains or plunges into deep ravines, or darts southward among a strange and wild people. . . ." Then the editor made a point with which Kendall too would have agreed: "The church needs just such indomitable pioneers at the front."

As for Jackson, the greatest front of all was to be Alaska.

CHAPTER 4

SHEPHERD TO A MIGHTY FLOCK

Jackson established the first Presbyterian mission in Alaska after many unsuccessful attempts had been made to get American denominations to send missionaries to the territory. Little was achieved in evangelization until his impetuosity and resolution made the difference between hope and reality, between fragmentary efforts and a permanent program.

The United States Army had been the principal representative of American authority in the possession for ten years after the purchase. In spite of the misconduct of some soldiers, there were those in the Army who played important roles in the establishment of Christian work among the Indians. One of these was Major General O. O. Howard, commander of the military department of the northwest, who had reported the need for missionaries in Alaska as early as 1871. Then in 1876 a group of Christian Indians from Metlakahtla in British Columbia came to Wrangell after being hired to cut wood for the Army. (Years later, Father William Duncan, the missionary to these Indians, climaxed a dispute with Church of England authorities by taking some of the Indians with him to Annette Island in southeastern Alaska where he established what was known then as New Metlakahtla and is now known as Metlakatla.) While working out their contract, these Christian Indians also carried on evangelization among the

Indians living in and around the settlement. When they had finished their contract and returned home, one of their number remained in Wrangell to work as a lay preacher. He needed help, however, and an Army officer stationed there assisted him in organizing a religious activity among the Wrangell Indians. Several wives of officers wrote to friends in the States imploring them to use their influence to get some church body to send a missionary to Wrangell.

About this same time, Jackson had asked his board to start mission work in Alaska. His suggestion was turned down because the territory was the responsibility of the foreign mission board. The Rev. A. L. Lindsley, minister of the Presbyterian Church in Portland, Oregon, asked the foreign board to undertake the work, but it was too much in debt and had too many other commitments to assume the responsibility. Lindsley finally took matters in his own hands. He found a volunteer to go to Alaska, but the man was forced to stop work after a few months because of ill health.

The immediate action that led to Jackson's work in Alaska came in the form of a letter written by an army private stationed at Wrangell, named J. S. Brown. The Army was about to leave the settlement in the spring of 1877 when Brown sent his all-important letter to General Howard:

"I write you hoping that you may be able and willing to assist these poor creatures in their endeavors to learn more of the good Saviour of whom they have learned but recently. Since the advent of the traders and miners among them, lewdness and debauchery have held high carnival, and the decimation of their numbers is the result. If a school and mission were established at Wrangell there would, no doubt, be an Indian population of over 1,000 souls located within reach of its benefits. . . . Can you not, will you not, make it your business to build up and foster this mission to Alaska? Send out a shepherd who may reclaim a mighty flock from the error of their ways, and gather them into the true fold."

Howard gave the Brown letter to Lindsley, who in turn gave it to a minister about to leave for a meeting of the General Assembly of the Presbyterian Church in Chicago. The clergyman met Jackson at the meeting and gave him Brown's letter. Jackson had it published in the Chicago *Tribune* and in a number of church publications, and again importuned the home mission board to do something about missionary work in Alaska. Fortunately, the Assembly authorized the home board to work among the natives in the western states and territories, an area reserved previously to the foreign board. It was assumed that while Alaska was not mentioned by name, the Assembly intended the territory to be included in the authorization, and the board assigned a man to go there. Once again, events had a way of working to Jackson's advantage. The minister selected for Alaska by the home board had already accepted another commission when this assignment reached him, and he elected to stay in the States. Then Kendall wrote a letter to Jackson that should have turned him away from Alaska but which, in the long run, served to head him in that direction. Jackson, of course, was eager to work there, but he had a number of unfulfilled obligations in the West, to which Kendall referred in the form of a mild rebuke:

"We [the mission board] think you have never done any thorough work in Montana. You have dashed in and out again. The church has come to demand something better. . . . No other part of your field seems to us so pressing in its demands at the present time. . . . You have explored New Mexico and Utah thoroughly, and Arizona considerably. . . . The time seems to us to come to do equally thorough and exhaustive work in Montana. . . . Then we want you [to go] to Corinne or Kelton [Nevada] . . . to Boise City and Walla Walla. . . ."

Kendall wanted Jackson to make a protracted survey, for there were candidates for the field and funds to support new work. Jackson noted at the bottom of this letter that the assignment "resulted in the opening of Alaska to gospel work." What he had in mind was his own work in the territory.

The manner in which it was begun illustrates the man's capacity to grasp opportunity and his preparedness to take great risks in order to achieve results. In spite of Kendall's desire for a survey of conditions and opportunities in Montana, reasonable circumstances limited the time available for the journey and forced its postponement. An Indian uprising in Idaho prevented Jackson from going there. Instead he went to Portland, Oregon, where he met an old friend, Mrs. Amanda McFarland. She and her late husband had been associates of his in the Southwest. Following her husband's death, she had moved to Portland where she became acquainted with Lindsley and shared his interest in Alaskan missionary needs. Jackson talked with both of them about missionary work, and learned that Mrs. McFarland was interested in working there herself. He explained to her that she would have to be prepared to risk the uncertainties of life in a strange land among a primitive people; in addition she would have to work without official recognition, for Jackson had no authority to organize mission work in Alaska. The fact of the matter is that Alaska at that moment was as far from the board's mind as anything could possibly be because of the interest in the American West. As soon as Jackson was convinced that Mrs. McFarland would do her best and was prepared to start to work at once, he made arrangements for the two of them to sail to Wrangell.

Wrangell was even more of a frontier community than Sitka. Most of its population of fifteen hundred were Indians. Jackson found there abundant evidence of the need reported by

Private Brown in his letter. Mrs. McFarland agreed to start a mission school while he promised to raise the necessary funds, and so the Presbyterians were launched in Alaska. When Jackson returned to New York, he discovered that the mission board was not pleased with what he had done. He explained that he felt there was not enough time to communicate with the board and get authorization for Mrs. McFarland and her work. The board decided that since the mission school had been organized, it would support Jackson's initiative. The situation was made more palatable by the fact that he was prepared to raise the funds required. He did such a good job that within two years he had received contributions totaling twelve thousand dollars.

During those two years, Mrs. McFarland struggled with problems that taxed her to the limits of her emotional and physical reserves. She wrote Jackson an unending stream of letters about her hopes and fears; she apprised him of financial difficulties, of the need for a doctor to aid the sick and a clergyman to organize a church. In one of her letters she included the plea of an Indian chief who was upset because his tribe was not being taught about Jesus, whereas several other tribes in the Wrangell area had received Christian instruction.

Not all of her letters were filled with fears and problems. One contained a long description of her first Christmas in Wrangell. She was awakened about one o'clock Christmas morning by a commotion outside her house. Hurrying to the window to investigate, she saw a crowd of Indians standing in the rain. Each one had an umbrella in one hand and a lantern in the other. When one of the Indians saw her at the window, he signaled to the others, and the crowd started to sing Christmas carols that Mrs. McFarland had taught them. Then they walked away and Mrs. McFarland returned to bed filled with new hope. While she was preparing breakfast that same morning, she again was aware of some unusual activity out-of-doors and, stepping outside, was stunned to see a crowd of about two hundred Indian men, women, and children. After her first surprise, she realized that the natives were preparing a Christmas greeting for her, and she called out "Merry Christmas" to them. A chorus of voices returned the greeting; then a small boy, dressed in a light blue suit with gilt stars pasted on the jacket, ran forward and spoke the lines that opened the ceremony. The Indians formed into a long line, their chief at the head, and moved toward the house. The chief stopped in front of Mrs. McFarland, wished her a Merry Christmas and before she knew what he intended, leaned forward and kissed her on the cheek. He stepped aside and, one by one, the others came forward to shake her hand and wish her joy.

A person who was less understanding of Mrs. McFarland's motives than Jackson, might have felt that she was a complainer, but he recognized her needs and sympathized with her anxieties. Many of her letters he published in the *Rocky Mountain Presbyterian* in order to arouse interest in her work. He reported her appeals for a doctor, another missionary, and a teacher, and her suggestion that Wrangell needed a home for native girls. He translated her goadings into his own arguments and prayers for the means and the men to do the work that was so urgent. Among those who responded to his call for assistance was the Rev. John Brady, who went to Alaska in 1878 as a missionary and remained there as a businessman and government official. Another was the Rev. S. Hall Young, who began a long and fruitful life in the territory when he joined Mrs. McFarland in Wrangell in August 1878.

There were occasions when events pushed Jackson faster than he intended to move, as was the case with the building of a home for girls at Wrangell. Early in 1878 Mrs. McFarland described her experience in rescuing a girl of thirteen who had been sold into slavery by her parents. The buyer was a white man and the price was twenty blankets. Blankets were the Indians' substitute for money, for which they had little use. The transaction appeared even more reprehensible than it was, and it made a deep impression on Jackson. He was already moved to action when another report from Mrs. McFarland arrived, dramatizing the need for a home for girls.

Upon entering the school one morning, she learned that two of the girls who attended her classes had been accused of being witches. They had been kidnaped and were being tortured at the Indian village. Her first impulse was to rush to their rescue even though the other pupils warned her that she might be killed for interfering with the ritual. Running toward the village, she heard the bedlam of the Indians who had drunk themselves into a frenzy and the terrified shrieking of their victims. They were bound to poles surrounded by a circle of about fifty men. The ring surged in and out as the dancers whirled and screamed and took turns slashing at the girls with razor-sharp knives. She hurled herself at the circle, not knowing how she would save the girls. The unexpectedness of her attack so startled the Indians that several drew back. One Indian lunged forward and knocked her to her knees, but her momentum carried her inside the ring. She turned to face the tormentors, arms outstretched in a pitiful effort to shield their victims. She pleaded and screamed in anger darting from one side of the circle to the other. One man made a half-hearted attempt to reach the girls, but he drew back when Mrs. McFarland ran toward him. The Indians understood little of what she shouted, but her appearance and the sound of her voice had their effect. The spell that held them was broken; one by one they slipped away. When the last Indian had disappeared, she took the girls back to Wrangell. Later during the night one of them was kidnaped a second time and murdered.

The story shocked Jackson and hastened his return to Alaska in 1879. Actually, there were several reasons for the trip. Kendall wanted to visit the new mission field. He and Jackson were to prepare a report for the Department of the Interior on conditions among the natives, a commission sought by Jackson to promote the trip over the objections of those who felt time and money were being wasted on Alaska. Then there was the need at Wrangell. Mrs. Jackson and Mrs. Kendall were members of the party.

Jackson's account of the difficulties in building the Wrangell home for girls illustrates the problems resulting from Alaska's remoteness:

"No one who has not tried building a thousand miles from a hardware store, a hundred miles from a sawmill, in a community where there is not even a horse, wagon or cart, and but one wheelbarrow, can realize the vexatious delays in such a work."

However vexatious, the home was completed. For a small number of Indian girls it became a sanctuary from the degrading effects of the illegal liquor traffic which haunted Jackson throughout the years he worked in Alaska. Some officials charged that the Army was responsible for introducing the Indians to whiskey. William G. Morris, a special agent for the United States Treasury Department, was of the opinion that while the higher army officers sought to control the importing of whiskey, the lower ranks did not. Morris claimed that "previous to the arrival of the military [whiskey] manufacture was unknown to the Indians, but no sooner had the soldiers made their appearance in Alaska than the detestable traffic commenced. . . . a whole race of prostitutes has been created. . . ."

William S. Dodge, collector of customs for Alaska, said that the Indians were not the only victims of drunkenness, for "many has been the night when soldiers have taken possession of a Russian house and frightened and browbeaten the women into compliance. . . . I have been called upon after midnight by men and women, Russian and Aleutian, in their night clothes, to protect them. . . . The conduct of some of the officers has been so demoralizing that it was next to impossible to keep discipline among the soldiers."

E. J. Baily, the medical director of the Army's Department of Alaska, made the point that the soldiers and Indians "mutually debauch each other, and sink into that degree of degradation in which it is impossible to reach each other through moral or religious influences."

It is pointless to blame the Army or any other single group for the existence of the liquor problem in Alaska, as John Brady did when he contended that "sending the soldiers [to Alaska] was the greatest piece of folly of which a government could be guilty." The frontier character of the territory and its isolation from centers of civil authority contributed at least as much to making liquor a disease from which all Alaskans suffered in one form or another. In the last analysis, Congressional inaction might be considered the prime cause. Jackson understood that the debauchery of all who were involved in the whiskey trade was inevitable, but he did not think the situation was beyond repair. He believed that good law enforcement and respect for the rights of the natives would overcome the effects of the traffic and put an end to it. This approach was confirmed by what had been accomplished among the Indians at Metlakatla whom he decided to visit in order to learn what he could about the nature and extent of the missionary work that had been done among them. He discussed the trip with Kendall. The two men agreed that

Kendall would remain in Wrangell to help with several problems while Jackson traveled the two hundred and fifty miles by water to Metlakahtla and the nearby community of Fort Simpson. Such a journey promised to be long and dangerous even in favorable weather, but by then the summer was already far enough advanced to produce storm and fog hazards that would increase the risks. Jackson's account of how he started the trip was that "while looking around, a large canoe came in from the Chilcat country loaded with furs and en route to Ft. Simpson. A portion of the crew were Christian Indians from Ft. Simpson, so there was no difficulty in arranging for a passage. Besides the six Christian Indians were twelve wild Chilcat savages headed by their medicine chief or schaman. Our canoe was about thirty-five feet long, five feet across and three feet deep." Jackson gives no explanation why the two groups of Indians were manning the canoe. The Christian Indians were Tsimpseans who spoke a different language, lived hundreds of miles south of the Chilcat country, and fought with the Chilcats at times.

The Indians left Wrangell the following day, with Jackson wedged into the center of the canoe, surrounded by furs, packs, and provisions. Late that afternoon, he saw a native village a short distance ahead along the shore; at the same time, he noticed that the Indians in the canoe were awe-stricken, absorbed in watching the settlement. When the canoe drifted abreast of the spot, Jackson decided that it was "a deserted village of the Stickines . . . only the coarse croak of the raven broke in upon the stillness and desolation." Crest poles leaned in every direction, the grotesque images that topped them outlined against the sky. The walls of the buildings had collapsed, though some of the corner posts were still in place. Huge floor beams, some sixty feet long and three to four feet thick, rested on a few posts. It was this ghostly reminder of the past that held Jackson's companions in awe. The mood passed, and at a sign from their medicine man, the Chilcats burst into a weird song whose cadence became the rhythm for the strokes of all the men in the canoe. When the Chilcats stopped their singing, the Tsimpseans joined in gospel hymns they had learned, and the paddlers picked up the new beat. Time and again during the trip the Indians would turn to song to relieve their weariness, for they seldom stopped either by day or night. Whenever it rained heavily—and on the occasions when they wanted to eat or take naps—they drove the canoe to shore to seek protection under the projecting rocks. For the most part, however, there was little shelter to be found; Jackson had to huddle under soggy blankets while the canoe plunged through rain and heavy seas. The weather became much worse the farther south they traveled, and for hours on end the canoe repeated the same pattern. The Indians would drive it to the crest of a wave where it would hang motionless for a second before plunging into the trough and rolling from side to side until the men drove it to the crest of the next wave. Jackson had to cling to the sides to keep his seat and crouched to avoid being soaked by the spray.

On the fifth day the sea was much calmer. But now a dense fog blotted out every landmark by which the Indians navigated, and the steersman, depending upon instinct alone, had to hold close to the shore. A blinding rain followed the fog, during which even the Indians were willing to seek shelter on shore. But after spending several hours under the poor protection of trees and rock ledges, they decided it would be better to continue on the water rather than remain cold and wet on land.

The storm broke at daylight, and later in the morning, the Indians cheered at the sight of the Metlakatla village. Jackson spent several days visiting the missions there and at Fort Simpson. He was pleased to meet Father William Duncan, the

Episcopal missionary who had converted the Tsimpseans. He also promised the Chilcats who had come south with him in the canoe that he would establish a mission and school for them in their own country hundreds of miles to the north on Lynn Canal. Having returned to Wrangell, he assisted Kendall in organizing eighteen Indians and five whites into the first Presbyterian church in Alaska; then after visiting Sitka both men returned to the States.

On the basis of his most recent experience in Alaska, Jackson prepared a report for the Treasury Department on the condition of the natives. He also prepared a lengthy memorandum for Carl Schurz, the Secretary of the Interior, to support Schurz' request that Congress appropriate funds for school work in Alaska. Congress had set aside fifty thousand dollars for schools in 1870, but because it had failed to provide the means of administering the funds, they were never used. There was little support for Schurz' request. Newspapers referred to Alaska as a "sucked orange," "an icehouse, a worthless desert." The statement made a few years earlier in a House Foreign Relations Committee minority report was still in vogue: Alaska would "be a source of weakness instead of power, and a constant annual expense for which there [would] be no adequate return . . . no capacity as an agricultural country . . . no value as a mineral country . . . its timber generally of poor quality and growing upon inaccessible mountains . . . its fur trade of insignificant value . . . the fisheries of doubtful value. . . ."

Jackson denied that there was any truth in such statements. He was convinced by observation that Alaska's resources were large and important. Others with sufficient professional training to evaluate Alaska's potential provided him with favorable analyses. He also argued that the proper development of these resources depended in part upon an educated native population. He reminded the federal administration that the national government received over a quarter of a million dollars in yearly rentals from the lease of the sealing rights on the Pribilof Islands. Part of the income, he contended, should be invested in a school system, for he felt that it would be wiser to spend a few thousands of dollars each year to civilize the natives than to spend far more trying to subdue them.

There was also the question of national reputation in his report to Schurz. Major General H. W. Halleck, speaking in the name of the United States Government, had promised that American teachers would be sent to Alaska to replace the Russian instructors who withdrew at the time of the purchase. General Howard and Indian Commissioner Vincent Colyer had repeated the promise. Jackson pointed out that the natives remembered and wanted to know when the promises would be redeemed. To show that they really desired help, he reported these words of an Alaskan Indian chief: "We ask of our father in Washington that we be recognized as a people . . . that we be civilized, Christianized, educated. Give us a chance and we will show to the world that we can become peaceable citizens and good Christians."

Jackson asked Schurz for funds to expand the Sitka mission school, after securing the approval of the Presbyterian home mission board, and to establish as many other like schools as the money would allow. He also addressed a memorial to the members of the House and the Senate, in which he again stressed the urgency of providing courses in the "common branches of an English education, the principles of a republican government, and such industrial pursuits as may seem best adapted to their circumstances." As long as the natives remained in ignorance, he warned, just so long would they practice polygamy, witchcraft, and slavery, and remain a burden to the white man.

Congress ignored Schurz' request, but Jackson did not lose

In August, 1885, the side-wheel steamer *Ancon* left Sitka, Alaska, without Sheldon Jackson, who was arrested at dockside and jailed by officials seeking to obstruct his work as U.S. agent for education. (p. 11)

Sitka, the territorial capital until 1906, had a more civilized appearance than most Alaskan settlements of the 1890's. At far right is the industrial training school Jackson helped to establish for Indian and Eskimo boys.

The Fourth of July, 1892: Jackson (*center*) lands the first reindeer from Siberia o the Alaskan coast near Port Clarence in an effort to save the Eskimos from starvatio and to provide them with the independence for a new way of life.

In 1892, Jackson photographed these Chuckchees of Siberia who sold him reindee for export to Alaska. Vigorous and friendly, the Chuckchees depended upon their rein deer for the hide on their tents and for food during the periodic famines which swep the Arctic on both sides of the Bering Sea.

The Siberian tribesmen (*above*) whom Jackson first brought to Alaska to handle the reindeer were often careless and lost many fawn; Jackson later sought the help of Laplanders (*below*) to teach animal husbandry to the Eskimos.

Jackson (*left*) stands before the school and reindeer station at Cape Prince of Wale
home base for W. T. Lopp (*second from left*) who, in 1897, drove hundreds of rein
deer a thousand miles to save 300 starving seamen at Point Barrow. (pp. 156-157)

Jackson (*left, wearing derby*) traveled often aboard the *Bear*, the U. S. Revenu
Cutter Service ship whose officers and crew were the "Good Samaritans" of Alaska: the
rescued the shipwrecked, aided the sick, landed food during famine, transported rein
deer, and helped to maintain the law.

Dutch Harbor, on Unalaska Bay in the Aleutians, was the site of another of Jackson's schools. From this area in 1894 the *Bear* rushed to the rescue of shipwrecked sailors stranded on Umnak Island to the east. (pp. 119-123)

A bleak and barren coastline ringed Plover Bay in Siberia where Jackson traveled in quest of reindeer. Mount Kennicott (*right*) was named for an American engineer.

December sunlight at Point Barrow, the northernmost Presbyterian mission station and a U. S. Government refuge for shipwrecked seamen.

Totem poles studded Indian settlements like the one at Wrangell, where, in 1877, Jackson founded the first Presbyterian mission in Alaska. The carvings represent clan or tribal crests.

Jackson on St. Lawrence Island in the Bering Sea, 1892, visiting a typical Eskimo congregation, which was startled by the sight of a camera.

Although years of hardship took their toll, Jackson never lost his determined expression and erect bearing. The Tsimpsean Indian boys from Metlakathlah (*above*) went with Jackson (*center*) and William Duncan (*right*), a Protestant Episcopal missionary, to enroll in the industrial school at Sitka in 1888. In 1905, four years before his death, he posed (*below*) with John G. Brady (*left*), the missionary who became Governor of Alaska, and William A. Kelly (*right*), School Superintendent of Southern Alaska.

The mission work pioneered by Sheldon Jackson moves swiftly forward today by air and sea. The *Arctic Messenger* (*above*) carries its missionary pilot to settlements scattered across thousands of miles of ice and snow on the North Slope of Alaska. The *Anna Jackman* (*below*), part of the Presbyterian "navy" in the 49th State, takes the gospel to isolated areas in the southeastern region.

hope or give up his efforts to get an appropriation. He became a one-man lobby in support of a better way of life for Alaska. He talked to anyone who would listen to his arguments about the need for doctors and teachers, better laws and effective enforcement, and adequate transportation facilities. He was recognized as an authority on the territory, and persons in and out of government listened to his views more than to anyone else's. But there were neither enough Congressmen who listened nor enough who were convinced to push legislation through Congress.

In 1880, in a fine example of interchurch co-operation, Jackson met with representatives of other denominations to work out a division of mission fields in Alaska. The Baptists undertook the development of Kodiak Island and the Cook Inlet region. The Episcopal Church was already at work in the Yukon and retained that region as its responsibility. The Methodists accepted the Aleutian and Shumagin Islands. The Moravians concentrated on the valleys of the Kuskokwim and Nushagak Rivers. The Congregationalists accepted the Cape Prince of Wales area. The Presbyterians kept the southeast as their major bailiwick while agreeing to start work at Point Barrow, which became the northernmost mission station in the world.

By July 1881 when he made his third trip to Alaska, Jackson was prepared to keep his promise to help the Chilcat Indians. But there was a problem of another kind there. Petty differences and personality conflicts were hampering Presbyterian work at Wrangell and had a deteriorating effect on other missions. It reached such proportions by the summer of 1881 that the missionary to the Chilcats, who had preceded Jackson to Wrangell, was fearful that the contention would hamper his work. On his arrival, Jackson wisely refrained from taking sides—Kendall had insisted that was the only sound course—and allowed the facts to assert themselves and end the bickering—at least for the time being. With this accomplished, he took the missionary and his family to a point 150 miles north of Sitka. This mission was known as Haines and, after overseeing the construction of a home, Jackson made a 500-mile canoe trip to visit other Indian villages in the southeast, then returned to the States.

CHAPTER 5

THE RIGHT MAN FOR THE JOB

The Presbyterian mission school at Sitka was beset by a number of difficulties during its first years. The Rev. John Brady first established the school in a log building that had been used as a Russian hospital and then as a barracks for American soldiers. It was in operation by the spring of 1878 but, in December of that year, it closed when the woman teacher married and left Sitka. Reopened in the fall of 1878, the years of its continuous service are dated from April 1880.

Fire destroyed the building in January 1882 and Jackson, then in the States, raised five thousand dollars to replace the structure. Upon his arrival in Sitka, he discovered that he had to find another source of lumber. So he bought a nearby cannery which had been destroyed when heavy snow collapsed the roof, floated the salvaged timber to Sitka, and constructed a two-story building, one hundred by fifty feet, on ground outside the village which was donated by Brady. This school was then known as the Sheldon Jackson Institute, not being officially named the Sitka Industrial and Training School until 1884. In 1885, the school was involved in the road-blocking controversy.

Sitka had been the most important settlement in the territory since its founding by a Russian trader named Aleksander Andreyevich Baranov. As it had been the center for Baranov's activities earlier, so it became the focal point for Jackson's participation in the later development of Alaska. Baranov and Jackson differed immensely in background and objectives, but their contributions to Alaska parallel each other in certain important areas. Both understood the territory's economic potential; both were concerned with protecting the native population. Baranov had been the chief resident director in Alaska for the Russian American Company, a fur-trading organization which was chartered by the Czarist government late in the eighteenth century. There had been a fair amount of fur trading in Alaska before then, but the Russian government had become concerned over the fact that individual traders were robbing and murdering the Indians. The company was chartered to bring order to Russia's trade with its North American possession and to eliminate the abuse of the natives, upon whom the company depended for gathering furs. Baranov, as company director, was charged not only with protecting the lives and property of the natives but with providing secular and religious instruction for them. The Russians had the obvious material motive in seeking to aid the Indians, but it was based on the belief that Alaska was a source of wealth, a fact that the American Congress was a long time in recognizing.

Baranov set about discharging his duties by building the fortified village of Old Sitka, or Fort Archangel Gabriel, in 1799. During his absence, Indians destroyed the place and killed or captured all its inhabitants. When he returned in 1804, Baranov subdued the Indians and then built a larger village several miles away. Modern Sitka grew upon the second site.

Baranov's word was law in Alaska. Jackson, on the other hand, had to depend on moral suasion to get results. His authority as a government official was limited in scope and constantly subject to criticism. Although interested primarily in the spiritual and educational welfare of the natives, he carried forward Baranov's belief in the economic importance of Alaska as well. Without any conscious effort to emulate the Russian, Jackson too stressed the value of aiding the Indians as part of that economic growth. Though he would have been the last to recognize it, Jackson's tendency was to be as unyielding as Baranov in the pursuit of his goals, with the result that he had to face much opposition.

After he had finished the job of rebuilding the Sitka training school in 1882, he returned to the States, spending the remainder of that year and most of 1883 discharging responsibilities not concerned with Alaska. He did take time to negotiate a contract with the Post Office Department for establishing a new mail service in the district. It was a canoe route manned by natives to serve communities in the southeast. Jackson went back to Alaska in 1884 as the manager of an excursion for delegates to a meeting of the National Education Association. It was during this visit that he merged Mrs. McFarland's home for girls with the school at Sitka after the Wrangell property had been destroyed by fire. He also helped to organize the First Presbyterian church in Sitka.

The year 1884 closed the first phase of his efforts in Alaska. Six Presbyterian missions were in operation by then, with seven missionaries on the field. Seventeen teachers had been recruited, and the mission-related school system had an enrollment of over five hundred students. All this resulted directly or indirectly from Jackson's efforts.

The second phase of his work in Alaska got under way that same year when Congress passed a law providing the territory with its first semblance of civil administration and appropriating twenty-five thousand dollars for a school system to be administered by a general agent for education under the

United States Bureau of Education of the Department of the Interior. The 1884 law has been criticized as a "composite of honest intentions, ignorance, stupidity, indifference, and quasi-expediency." While its author, Senator Benjamin Harrison, admitted that the law was weak and ineffectual in spots, he insisted that it was the best that Congress would enact. Harrison was probably correct. With respect to Jackson's career as agent for education, the measure was deficient in that it failed to provide adequate means of enforcing the criminal code, which was based on the legal system in the Oregon Territory. This deficiency became a source of the difficulties soon to beset the missions and the schools. It was poor enforcement of the laws which led the missionaries and their supporters to agitate for the elimination of the liquor traffic and related abuses, bringing the church element into sharp conflict with secular interests in the territory. Jeannette Nichols points out that the prospectors and young businessmen in Alaska did not advocate drunkenness. They just wanted the missionaries to talk less of it. "They feared that every time statements appeared in print referring to Indians and prohibition in Alaska, capital was frightened away and immigration was discouraged."

But there were other factors which discouraged investment and limited the territory's population increase. One of them was pointed out years later by James Wickersham, a long-time Alaskan delegate to Congress: "It is a sad commentary upon the patriotism of our American Congress that there actually exists today [in 1923] a congressional government in Alaska more offensively bureaucratic in its basic principles and practices than that which existed . . . during the seventy years of Russian rule under the Czar. A careful study of the Russian-American charter of 1844, and the bureaucratic rules and regulations for the government of Russian America under that charter, when compared with the present government in Alaska, by executive proclamations and rules and regulations of more than thirty American bureaus, will amaze an American student at the comparative simplicity and reasonableness of the Russian system."

Early in 1885, before Jackson was named agent for education, Governor Kinkead wrote John Eaton, Commissioner for Education in Washington, that there were several locations where children were "crazy to have schools. The people have the money and are willing to pay teachers if they can procure them. [But you] cannot combine Indian and white schools. People are generally friendly to the missionaries and do not wish to interfere with their work among the Indians. . . . I think it would be unwise, certainly unpopular, to place the [school work] in the hands of the missionaries. These things should be in charge of the state or territorial authorities rather than in the charge of one particular sect."

Eaton understood the thinly veiled charge in Kinkead's letter. He informed the governor that there was no evidence that the Presbyterians had been favored more than other denominations with government support for their schools. He further pointed out that the various denominations working in Alaska were anxious to "co-operate in the work of establishing schools" and that they understood they had to be nonsectarian in their instruction. Eaton did not tell Kinkead that he felt the mission stations were the only dependable contacts for organizing a school system and that the churches would make substantial contributions of their own to the schools.

In the midst of the discussion over who was to administer the schools and how the work was to be carried on, Jackson was appointed general agent for education early in 1885. At the same time, Haskett was in the process of planning and executing his schemes to destroy the Sitka industrial school and discredit Jackson. With the failure of these plans and the arrival in Sitka of the men who replaced Haskett, McAllister, and company, it looked for a while as if harmony had come at last. Unhappily, this was not the case. How much responsibility for the failure to co-operate rests upon Jackson and how much upon the new federal officials is a question that must be examined on the basis of the facts.

Alfred P. Swineford, who replaced Kinkead as governor, was an aggressive advocate of more self-government for Alaska. During his four years in office, he worked diligently on behalf of small business, mine operators, and, apparently, the Indians. Jackson's inability to get along with Swineford illustrates how he may have permitted his personal dislikes to prevent an association that could have produced greater advantages to Alaska than either was able to produce by himself. Jackson made inquiries into Swineford's background in the States and the replies received from a clergyman, a couple of bankers, and a businessman cast aspersions on his character and questioned his integrity. Unless Jackson had other information to support the charges that were retailed to him—and he cited none—it stands against him as evidence of a lack of charitableness that he permitted such charges to color his attitude toward the governor. It was a regrettable situation and the possibility of any future close collaboration between the two was lost. It is not clear whether Swineford knew of Jackson's investigation, but in February 1886 he wrote to a woman in Washington, D.C., who was extremely active in support of Alaskan missionary work. The letter was an obvious effort to undermine Jackson's position, for Swineford went out of his way to praise the work of other missionaries in Alaska and to describe his own visits to Indian settlements where he found a desire for schools. He promised the woman that he would fill the Sitka industrial home with "all the native pupils it could possibly accommodate."

Swineford also discussed Jackson's differences with the first set of Alaskan officials. He wrote that he was "more than ever convinced that [he] was right in ascribing to Dr. Jackson's want of discretion—to use no harsher expression—in large part the troubles which beset your missions in Alaska last year [1885]. These troubles are practically ended, but I very much fear their renewal should Dr. Jackson be sent back in any official capacity in connection with the missions or industrial school. In my opinion his return would be a sad mistake inasmuch as it would militate against, rather than promote, the success of the efforts you are making for the moral and educational welfare of the natives. I offer this suggestion in all candor, and most certainly through no feeling of enmity to Dr. Jackson for whom I sincerely hope you may be able to find employment in a field where his zeal and energy will be better appreciated. . . ."

The effort to undermine Jackson shifted from Swineford's oblique approach to the direct attack which appeared in the New York *World* in March 1886. A dispatch ascribed to the newspaper's Washington correspondent charged that Jackson was a "hypocrite, a liar, and a dishonest, designing man and an arrant rogue." The article said that he had lied about the number of schools that existed in Alaska and had boasted that he had "eighteen United States Senators at his beck and call." It is no wonder that Jackson wrote to President Cleveland that "the number and character of misstatements sent out from Alaska concerning my work is something wonderful. . . ." It was actually something less than wonderful.

At his friends' urging, Jackson answered the newspaper's allegations for his own protection, explaining that he had named only the seven places where schools were located—Juneau, Sitka, Wrangell, Jackson, Hoonah, Haines and Unalaska—no more and no less. He admitted having said that he knew some legislators but added that he had merely told "disheartened teachers and missionaries that [he] knew of Christian and honorable men in the United States Senate who were interested in Alaska and the welfare of its people, who would not stand by and see the work so well commenced, destroyed by bad officials . . . and that when the facts should become known in Washington, there would be a change of officials."

No doubt he was intending to assure the missionaries and teachers that their efforts would not be wasted, but it is hard to understand how a man like Jackson could have been so naïve as to expect his opponents to take a calm, dispassionate view of his words. Jackson was well aware that the opposition resented his association with people of influence in Washington and, in particular, his efforts to effect the removal of Alaskan officials. Even those who were neutral were not always pleased with his "interference" in Alaska's internal affairs. His blind spot was that he took it for granted no one would question the sincerity of his motives. It did not seem to occur to him that his antagonists would judge him by their own standard of conduct or that others might feel he was overbearing.

There may have been another cause for resentment of which Jackson was completely unaware. His association in the States with persons of intellectual stature may have served to emphasize to him the comparative mediocrity of many who held federal posts in the district and would not have served to improve his relationships with them.

There was one clear reason for resentment: his intolerance where moral issues were concerned, and the feeling of many that the church group had a holier-than-thou attitude toward other Alaskans. Jackson never approved of compromise between right and wrong, nor between what he believed to be in the best interest of a particular situation and what he considered inimical to it. Many persons—and not just Alaskans and Alaskan officials—thought him an unreasonable man.

Swineford saw only one side of his nature, just as Jackson saw only one side of the governor, and it is regrettable that the two were not able to lay aside their differences and combine their best qualities in a common effort. That they might have been able to complement one another is supported by Ernest Gruening's description of Swineford as a man of energy, courage, and vision, who was not appointed governor in 1893 because of the opposition resulting from his "fearless espousal of what he deemed was in the public interest."

Jackson also suffered from opposition growing out of his insistence on running the schools in a manner he felt to be compatible with the good of all. A Sitka grand jury revived the 1885 charges against him and complained further that he was not doing a good job of administering the schools. The grand jury asked for his dismissal. Commissioner Eaton wasted no time in rejecting the imputation that Jackson was incompetent and unfamiliar with Alaska's school needs. Eaton said that Jackson had "done more than any other one man to make the condition of [Alaska] known to the people of the United States and to create the sentiment out of which has come the legislation to establish a government for that neglected country. . . . In his conferences with us, he has shown a ready appreciation of the fact that education . . . should not be exclusively in letters, but specially adapted to the people in their environment and fitted to prepare them most speedily to improve their condition to make them intelligent, virtuous, industrious and skillful in the pursuit of their various avocations and in the discharge of their duties to each other as citizens of the country now responsible for their government."

These attacks are important more because they obscured the fundamental difficulties in organizing and operating the schools than for their effect on Jackson. Several unusual problems requiring the most objective approach faced the agent for education in Alaska. One was the difficulty of making an equitable distribution of educational facilities among the white and native children. Another arose out of the desire of Alaskans to participate more fully in the administration of their schools. A third pertained to the vastness of the country. There were other unresolved issues, but these three were basic to the conflict that raged over the schools. The question of local school control and geography would have presented a barrier to any school administrator; in the case of Jackson, they served to maintain the opposition to him.

There is no question about his deep concern over the lack of schools for native children, and he was too aware of the shameful treatment accorded the American Indian to have any illusions about the attitude of the whites toward Alaska's aborigines. As a Presbyterian minister as well as a government official, he was convinced of the need for bringing Christian influence to bear upon the natives. Hence the Protestant white population feared he would slight their children for Indian youth; persons of Russian origin were concerned that education would be Presbyterian. The fear was unjustified since there were five or six other church groups who also operated schools and because the government schools were far from being staffed exclusively by Presbyterians. Jackson's superiors called attention to these facts whenever the charge was repeated that one denomination had a monopoly over the school system. However, there were those who believed that being Presbyterian was a prerequisite to getting an appointment in a school under Jackson's administration.

The claim that he deliberately administered the school law to the disadvantage of the whites had little justification in fact, but any lack of facilities in schools for whites as compared to those in schools for Indians could result in no other impression than that Jackson was being partial. The person who reported on the background to Jackson's arrest on the *Ancon* also provided an analysis of the relative school needs of white and Indian children:

"The newly-appointed governor [Swineford] reports about 1,900 white inhabitants in the southern part of the territory. As many of these are white men without families, the number of children of school age must be small. Hence, the present requirements for white schools can only be quite limited, and are needed, I would presume, at only Wrangell, Juneau, and Sitka. . . . The schools already established, we were led to believe, were well cared for and doing good work, being fairly well conducted and meeting with no special opposition. The work of the Indian schools is necessarily much larger and more difficult, and yet with all the ordinary difficulties, there are special advantages in teaching the Alaskan Indians. . . . The schools for these children at Wrangell and Sitka seemed well managed, and certainly have very competent and even consecrated teachers, doing their work well and thoroughly."

One of the first population estimates for Alaska, made in 1883, put the whites at 6,500 as against more than 8,000 Creoles (Russian fathers and native mothers), Aleuts, and civilized natives, plus 35,000 uncivilized aborigines. The more accurate 1890 census placed the white population at 4,300 out of a total of 32,000. The disproportion between whites and natives was far less in southeast Alaska than in the territory as a whole. Juneau, for example, had 671 whites out of a total of 1,253 in 1890. It was natural that the claim of unfair treatment of white children should stem largely from the southeast.

While the whites were not opposed to providing schools for the natives, to satisfy their demands would have pre-empted a far larger portion of the available funds than could have been justified.

Jackson handled the racial problem in the schools by providing separate facilities in areas where there were relatively large numbers of white students, but in general he spent the larger part of the school funds to meet the greater needs of the natives. This was not the most prudent approach, but it was fair, in addition to being courageous.

The problem that arose from Alaska's great size was complicated by the fact that the inhabitants of one region were strangers to those of another, and each section had its peculiar needs. The extreme weather in the Arctic sharply limited the number of months when Jackson could work there. July and August were the most favorable months, but then the people in the southeast felt he ought to be at work among them. Individual schools were located four to six thousand miles from his administrative headquarters in Washington and from one hundred to fourteen hundred miles from each other. Building materials and classroom equipment had to be transported forty-five hundred miles in some instances. It was necessary to take most roundabout routes to travel from one point in the territory to another, involving hundreds of wasted miles, while direct passage from Sitka to other settlements was very irregular.

The issue arising from the desire of Alaskans to participate more in the control of the schools was related to the geography of the territory. Jackson deprecated the fact that Washington tried to apply school systems existing in the States to a region with completely different needs. He preferred decentralization for the sake of efficiency and to encourage greater local participation. But once again, the nature of the region worked against him. He supported the creation of three school districts—Sitka, Kodiak, and Unalaska. Sitka was to comprise an area of 29,000 square miles; Unalaska, 431,545; and Kodiak, 70,000. Each of the districts was to have its own deputy superintendent, with Jackson responsible for securing equipment and co-ordinating the work. He planned to sit on the Sitka district committee, along with the governor and federal judge. The district committees for Kodiak and Unalaska were to consist of the deputy superintendent, the United States commissioner, and the deputy collector of customs.

The plan did not work well for a number of reasons. It was difficult, in the first place, to get the right men to fill the federal posts, and those of lesser ability were not the men to run a school district. Because transportation was limited and expensive, committee members had to live in the same community if they were to meet as often as necessary. Yet when that was the case, the committee acquired a local rather than a regional aspect, with the result that when good measures were proposed, the rivalries existing among communities made it impossible to put them into practice. Jackson later favored the creation of town school boards to be appointed locally. That failed because there were no funds to pay the members of the committees, and people were not willing to serve without pay.

In the face of all these problems, Washington continued to believe that Jackson was doing a good job as general agent. It was, therefore, inevitable that an impasse should develop over the administration of the schools. Alaskans were not satisfied, but their government did not believe they were justified in their complaints. It might have been possible to cut the knot by dismissing Jackson, but that involved questions of principle. Certainly no one but a man moved by a deep desire to aid in the development of the territory would have put up with the frustrations which he endured. Fortunately, he had friends who demonstrated their belief in him and in what he was trying to do. One of these supporters was William C. Norcross, of Monmouth, Illinois. Norcross wrote a letter to Congressman William H. Neece in 1886 which sums up much of what there is to say about certain aspects of Jackson's Alaskan career, although the letter implies a political motivation on his part that did not exist:

"... from a purely political standpoint, we can gain nothing by having [Jackson] removed, because he had been of considerable service in ousting the old Republican officials out of office in Alaska. His father, who lives in Galesburg, is one of the most uncompromising Democrats I ever knew and had been for more than twenty years to my certain knowledge. My idea is that although Dr. Jackson on war issues was inclined to act with the Republicans, that nevertheless there is enough Democracy in him to make him all right now. But there is one thing I am certain about, and that is that he is a man of such unquestioned integrity and ability, and he has so much influence both in church and state, that I believe he can't be put out, as a matter of fact. But even if he could be put out, I don't have any idea that we can find a man in the country who *can*, if he would, discharge the duties of the office so well. The chances are that, if he were to be put out of office, it would raise such a howl, as would hurt our party from Maine to Georgia, because [he] is well-known by all the church men and prominent educators in the country. It is absolutely true of him, *that he is the right man for the job*. He has been engaged in that kind of work most of his life. . . . I know him intimately for more than twenty years and know that he is pre-eminently qualified for the place he fills which is under the supervision of the Department of the Interior. He is in every sense of the word a reliable, competent and efficient man."

When Gruening looked at what was achieved in Alaska under American ownership during the nineteenth century, he concluded that "much of the progress in assimilating the native to the white culture was due to the early missionary effort, transformed in part after 1884 into a federally conducted educational system, which, despite its chronic insufficiency of appropriations, represented till the end of the century the only evidence of governmental interest in the people of Alaska." Jackson was both the spearhead of that early missionary effort and the administrator of the federally conducted system, and Gruening saw fit to say that *the people* of Alaska —not just one group—were the beneficiaries of his efforts.

CHAPTER 6

DEATH STALKS THE ESKIMOS

Sheldon Jackson's major achievement in Alaska, if not in his entire career, was that he saved the Eskimos from extinction.

The plight of the Arctic natives stemmed from the fact that they were unable to cope with the effects of the white man's presence in the territory. Their society was simple and uncomplicated, reinforced by a climate which imposed on all the need for a high degree of mutual trust and co-operation. Their way of life was built largely around the whale and the walrus, which provided them with food, clothing, fuel, and materials for making homes, boats, implements, and hunting weapons. To a lesser degree, the caribou and other fur-bearing land animals also supplied their needs.

With the coming of the white man, however, the whale and the walrus were hunted almost to the point of decimation, and his rifle drove the caribou herds into regions inaccessible even to the Eskimos. The white man also brought with him whiskey, prostitution, and illnesses to which the natives had no resistance and little defense. The worst of their situation was that few white people considered the Eskimos worth the effort it would take to help them. As the nineteenth century grew longer, their future grew shorter. Thousands of them had been living along the north and northwest coasts of

Alaska in the 1820's, but they were numbered in the hundreds by the 1880's. Nuwuk, once a village of about a thousand, had dwindled to less than one hundred by the time Jackson arrived in Alaska. Point Franklin, which had been the site of a good-sized community during the first part of the nineteenth century, had become little more than a name. Only three families remained of the one to two thousand natives who had dwelt along Shishmaref Inlet. The death rate among the tribes of the coastal area between Point Barrow and Point Hope had jumped so far beyond the birth rate that they had virtually disappeared.

When all these facts became known to Jackson, he recognized that the Eskimos were doomed unless someone made a sound, long-range effort to save them. His plan was twofold: the introduction of Siberian domesticated reindeer into Alaska to provide a new source of food and a new economy, and the establishment of schools where the Eskimos could learn new trades and find support in their struggle against the debilitating effects of the white man's less admirable qualities. He succeeded in both endeavors, and the magnificence of his achievement lies in the fact that he did so almost singlehandedly in the face of constant ridicule and opposition.

It may appear to those who see Jackson only as a missionary that his efforts on behalf of the Eskimos were relatively unimportant. To be sure, the number of those who became Christians as a result of the importation of the reindeer is out of proportion to the time and money he expended. Those who deprecate his success in protecting the material well-being of the Arctic natives and emphasize his missionary achievements must understand that Jackson's dedication to Christian principles transformed the reindeer work from a venture in social welfare into an act of faith. He believed in the Christian's responsibility as a citizen to help others escape the shackles of fear and the bondage of want. He believed in the right of all men to enjoy the best possible life. He was more concerned with putting faith into practice then in getting evidence of Christian commitment from the Eskimos. Evangelization was important to him, but he was aware of the prior need for giving the natives evidence of what Christianity means in practice. He knew that "faith without works is dead, being alone."

Great vision was required to save the Eskimos, and the tenacity to make that vision a reality. But Jackson was particularly fortunate in having the co-operation of the Revenue Cutter Service of the United States Treasury Department. This government agency had performed an unheralded mission in Alaska from the time of the purchase; often it was the only evidence of American justice and authority in the territory. It enforced the law against poachers and the smugglers of illegal whiskey, provided food for starving natives, and medical care for the injured, the sick, and the diseased at remote places along the coast. Hundreds of shipwrecked sailors owed their lives to the rescue work of the Revenue Service, whose officers were policemen and good Samaritans, friends and counselors. With no other group of men in Alaska did Jackson have a stronger bond, apart from the missionaries and the teachers. Their relationship developed out of a mutual respect for one another's courage and devotion to duty beyond official requirements. The revenue steamers were Jackson's outposts, and the men who commanded them were his eyes and ears and hands, reaching out to far-flung schools and mission stations.

The revenue officer closest to him was Captain M. A. Healy, commander of the steamer *Bear*, which he used as home and office for months at a time while cruising in northern waters. Healy was interested in more than upholding the law, for he believed in the right of the natives to protection. He agreed with Jackson on the need for helping them acquire new skills so as to be able to compete in the white man's world. And he abhorred the whiskey trade and its effect upon all who were involved in it.

Among the reports that Jackson received from the Revenue Service about conditions in remote areas, there was one that disturbed him particularly and spurred him to action. It was the account of a visit by a revenue ship to St. Lawrence Island, located at the southern entrance to the Bering Strait, during the summer of 1888. Such visits were always the occasion for rejoicing among the natives, but on this occasion there was no one to greet the landing party. The reason became clear when the men reached the native village: everyone was dead. A check of conditions turned up empty whiskey bottles but no furs or ivory of any value. The same scene was repeated at the next two villages visited by the revenue men, and it was not until they called at a settlement on the southern side of St. Lawrence Island that the cause of the disaster was known. White traders had come to the island and traded whiskey for whalebone, walrus tusks, and furs. The natives in the three upper settlements had then gone on a drinking spree which lasted through the weeks when they should have been hunting and fishing. The few who made an effort to get food were in such poor physical condition from the effects of the whiskey that they brought back only enough for day-to-day needs and nothing to stockpile against the coming winter. As a result, four hundred men, women, and children died, most of them from starvation. Only a few survived. The fourth village escaped the fate of the others because the traders ran out of whiskey and did not stop there.

Jackson wrote a long memorandum to the Commissioner for Education, urging the immediate establishment of schools among the Eskimos. He also published a series of newspaper articles on living conditions in the Arctic and subarctic to explain that the natives were in danger of dying out if help was not provided soon. Stressing the importance of religious and secular education, he advertised in the religious press for "Christian teachers for mission schools" with the warning that "the rigors of the Arctic winter and the self-denial and patience" that were required should make volunteers think twice before offering their services. "None other will succeed," he wrote, "or be willing to remain there even if sent." The results were amazing. Twenty-four men and women applied for the positions. Of these he selected four men—one to work at Point Hope, another at Point Barrow, and two at Cape Prince of Wales. The Bureau of Education was only able to provide travel funds and money for school supplies and building materials. Jackson, therefore, appealed to the churches to underwrite the salaries of the four instructors and received guarantees of support.

At the same time that he urged the establishment of the three new schools. Jackson outlined his plan to bring reindeer to Alaska. The Department of the Interior gave tentative approval and instructed him to collect data to support a formal recommendation upon which affirmative action could be taken. He asked for the assistance of the Revenue Cutter Service and was authorized to make the trip on the *Bear*. Having arranged to meet the four new teachers in Alaska later in the summer, he left for the west coast to join the revenue steamer.

The timing of his request for transportation was fortuitous because Healy was then under orders to visit the half-civilized Koriaks in the vicinity of Cape Navarin in Siberia. Several years earlier, a number of whaling vessels had been crushed by the ice in the Bering Sea. An American seaman who survived was found by the Koriaks and nursed to health; he remained with the Cape Navarin natives for over two years before he was found and returned to the States. Congress voted to reward the Siberians, and Healy had the job of delivering one thousand dollars in gifts to them. It was such a strange assortment of items that Healy must have felt he was running a general store instead of commanding a revenue steamer. There were hundreds of yards of cotten material, needles, looking glasses, bread, sugar, tea, molasses, pails, pans, iron pots, a wide variety of carpentry tools, rifles, shot guns, cartridges, caps, shot, powder, lead, axes, knives, fur traps, pipes, tobacco, snuff, goggles, beads, and a box of toys.

While Healy distributed the gifts, Jackson had no trouble finding facts to support his contention that the possession of domesticated reindeer was responsible for the sound economy of the Siberian tribes. The animal furnished food when hunting and fishing were insufficient. Its hide was used for clothing and housing material, and the bones were made into implements. When famine struck Siberian tribes which did not keep reindeer, they were often able to escape starvation by purchasing reindeer meat from those who did. Jackson was of the opinion that the Koriaks' good-naturedness derived, at least in part, from their sense of security, and he was impressed by their healthy and athletic appearance. The men shaved the crown of their heads, allowing a fringe of coarse, black hair to hang down over the forehead and ears. It gave a monklike appearance to their broad, flat faces. The women parted their hair in the middle and plaited it into two long braids that hung down the back. Some wore strings of colored beads, others had pendants in their ears. Almost every woman had tattooing down the center of the forehead, along each side of the nose, and on the cheeks. Some men and women were also tattooed on the arms and hands.

Despite their friendliness, none of the herders showed any interest in selling reindeer. Even though the *Bear* visited other points along the coast, Jackson was still unable to find a native who would trade his animals. Otherwise, however, the trip was a success, for it gave him confidence that the importation of reindeer would give the Eskimos in Alaska a new lease on life. In his formal request for approval and funds, he pointed out that "the sea could not be restocked with whale as a stream [could] be restocked with fish. To feed the [people] at government expense would pauperize and in the end would as certainly destroy the [Eskimos]." He reasoned that the introduction of reindeer would "do more than preserve life. It will preserve the self-respect of the people and advance them in the scale of civilization. It will change [them] from hunters to herders. It will also utilize the hundreds of thousands of square miles of moss-covered tundra of Arctic and sub-Arctic Alaska and make these now useless and barren wastes conducive to the wealth and prosperity of the United States. To reclaim and make valuable vast areas of land, otherwise worthless; to introduce large, permanent, and wealth-producing industries, where previously none had existed; to take a barbarian people on the verge of starvation and lift them up to a comfortable self-support and civilization is certainly a work of national importance."

Jackson made one other proposal in connection with his plan for the Eskimos. He urged the Department of the Interior to get Congress to extend to Alaska the provisions of an act authorizing the establishment of governmental experiment stations for the American Indians. He believed that if such facilities were available, the Eskimos could be trained in agricultural and mechanical arts.

His first trip to Siberia ended in time to meet the schooner transporting the four teachers and the building materials for the new schools. The two ships met at Cape Prince of Wales where construction was started on a schoolhouse on July 4 and completed in eight days. This was the first mission station and school on the barren coast of the Seward Peninsula. The men who were stationed there were William Lopp and H. R. Thornton. The *Bear* next stopped at Point Hope, two hundred and fifty miles to the north, a journey that took Jackson past a bleak and sparsely inhabited coast, the graveyard of countless whaling vessels. Heavy fog shrouded the area during the two and one-half months when the ice pack receded from shore allowing whaling vessels to sail north. But there was always the threat of a sudden shift in the wind which would drive the ice back toward land. A few years before Jackson passed up the coast in the *Bear*, thirty-three ships had been caught in the ice, stranding more than twelve hundred men who were lucky to escape with just their lives.

Construction on the Point Hope schoolhouse was advanced sufficiently by July 21 for the teacher, John Driggs, who was also a medical doctor, to live in it while he supervised the completion of the work. Jackson took time while at Point Hope to inspect a nearby settlement where the natives lived in underground houses, for he was always eager to see anything new or different. The home he visited was entered through a square opening at ground level that was so small it was a tight squeeze even for him. A long, narrow passageway extended from the bottom of the opening into two large rooms, each big enough for a family of ten persons. A platform-like structure skirted three sides of each room. Against the fourth wall there was a stone two feet long with a shallow depression on the upper side which served as a combination stove and lamp. The natives used whale oil for fuel and a wadding of tundra moss for a wick.

The inhabitants of the houses were "as dirty in their habits" as any people Jackson had seen. But they appeared to him to be "bright and docile," and he was convinced that "something could be made of them if they [had] a chance." Some of them wore reindeer furs, others had coats made of the skins of birds which had been tanned with the feathers in place.

The last leg of the journey to Point Barrow was through a dangerous three-hundred-mile stretch of ocean. Frequently, the *Bear* had to be anchored to ice floes because its progress was blocked. Each time the ice pack opened, the steamer would move farther north. A cold, wet wind lashed the ship throughout the seven-day trip to Barrow, the northernmost inhabited spot on the continent. Leander Stevenson was the teacher stationed there. It was fortunate that he did not realize how frustrating life would be there, or he might have remained on board the *Bear* and gone back home.

Jackson returned to the States immediately after the establishment of the new schools in the hope that Congress would authorize a reasonable sum of money for inaugurating the reindeer project. But Congress balked. Senators who were sympathetic to the plan supported a fifteen-thousand-dollar figure, but the House would not agree, perhaps under the influence of skeptics who condemned the idea as far too expensive. Some argued that the Siberians would not sell animals because of their superstitions, while others contended the animals would not survive transportation or be able to live on Alaska's tundra moss. In general, those who objected labeled the proposal as another of Jackson's schemes to make something out of heathens who could not be changed.

His superiors then approved a proposal to raise funds privately, and with two thousand dollars secured by such means, he boarded the *Bear* at Seattle on the morning of May 30, 1891. The purpose of this trip was to make the annual tour of inspection and then return to Siberia. On this voyage as well as every subsequent one on the revenue steamer, Jackson kept a daily record of weather conditions, temperatures at specific hours, wind direction, flora and fauna, geographical and historical information. To which he added descriptions that would embellish any travel book and reports on social and economic problems in Alaska.

As the steamer headed up Puget Sound, he became very seasick. But he was sufficiently recovered by the time the vessel reached the Swedish Lutheran mission at Yakutat to go ashore and visit the spot. The *Bear* resumed the trip in such clear weather that Mt. St. Elias stood out sharp and clear seventy miles away. The mountain range that paralleled the coast had peaks that towered close to twenty thousand feet, some appearing to rise right out of the water. Blue-white glaciers spread across the valleys between the mountains and back into the interior. At other places deep carpets of evergreen trees stretched from the foot of the range almost to the water's edge. Nearer Mt. St. Elias was another group of glaciers thousands of feet deep and more than a hundred miles in length, forming perhaps the largest glacial system outside the polar cap. In this area Healy sought an anchorage from which to land a survey party working under the joint auspices of the United States Geological Office and the National Geographic Society. The captain found a sheltered cove, but before sending the survey group ashore with its equipment, he sent in an exploring party to make certain that the beach could be reached safely. When they had received an all-clear signal, two loaded cutters left the *Bear*. The first negotiated the slightly heavy surf without any difficulty; but the second capsized, and six of the seven men in it were drowned, including two members of the expedition. This tragedy ended efforts to send supplies ashore; the remainder of the day was spent in a fruitless search for the missing men until it became too dangerous. The following morning, another cutter went as close to shore as possible to open communications with the crewmen who had spent the night on the beach. It was learned that two bodies had been washed up on shore. One was buried on land and the other, that of an officer of the *Bear*, was eventually returned to the steamer. The remaining supplies were landed at slack tide until another cutter capsized, but with no loss of life. The survey party was finally landed the following day, and the steamer returned to Sitka where Jackson conducted a funeral service for the men who had been lost.

From Sitka the revenue steamer headed north once more, bound for Cape St. John on the Alaska Peninsula. Jackson was spellbound by the magnificence of the view:

"Hour after hour I sat watching with unabated interest the ever-changing panorama. To the south, Castle Rock and, beyond that, Big and Little Koniski Islands. In front was Andronick Island and between [it] and Nagai Island the Seven Haystack Rocks stood sentinel across the north half of the straits. Over and beyond them was the main peninsula with its snow-covered mountains glistening in the morning sun. In the lower ravines lay great banks of fog. . . . To the right of us a school of whales is blowing. Then a sea otter tantalizingly lifts his head from his watery house to see what strange monster is passing by. . . ."

A small but important incident occurred when Jackson reached Dutch Harbor to inspect the school located there. A few days before his arrival a drunken native woman had taken her child from the school. As soon as he knew of the woman's action, Jackson asked the United States Commissioner to effect the child's return. When the woman barricaded her home, he had the door knocked in and the child removed. The affair served notice on everyone that Jackson would not tolerate interference with the operation of the schools nor allow anyone to obstruct their prime purpose, namely, to train native children to live in a world that was changing rapidly.

Beyond Dutch Harbor were Alaska's two great seal rookeries, St. Paul and St. George Islands, also known as the Pribilof Group. The islands were under the control of the Alaska Commercial Company by the terms of a twenty-year lease from the federal government. Between 1870 and 1890 the company netted eighteen million dollars for its fourteen stockholders, but during the last years of its lease, it had taken so many undersized seal pelts that the herds were reduced in number to a dangerously low level. A Treasury Department agent in 1890 reported such extensive damage that it would take an indefinite number of years for the herds to return to normal size. Earlier reports by other agents had given no indication of what was taking place, which in itself was an indication of the control that outside business interests exerted on law enforcement in Alaska. The company was also responsible for the welfare of the natives who lived on the islands; but just as early reports had omitted mention of the declining seal population, so they glossed over the conditions of the natives. The actual state of affairs came to light when special Treasury agent Joseph Murray reported a flagrant disregard for the health of the natives. He claimed that there was a complete absence of toilet facilities in one village where the waste drained into the only source of drinking water. Children on St. George Island who had been attending the company-operated school for seven years were still unable to speak or read English. Conditions on St. Paul Island were no better. To forestall any claim that the natives were incapable of learning, Murray cited the case of six little girls, taken from the "poorest, lowest, dirtiest, and most ignorant" of the Pribilof natives. The children were placed in the mission school at Unalaska, and in two years they were able to write "English as well as the average white school child of similar age." Reports such as this convinced Jackson of the great need that had to be met here and documented his contention that Alaska's natives were often treated with great callousness.

The 1891 trip almost came to an abrupt and tragic end on July 4 when the revenue steamer neared the southeast coast of St. Lawrence Island. The ship had been sailing due west, but because of the heavy fog she was kept barely under way. During the night of July 3, however, a strong easterly drift carried her so close to the island that with the lifting of the fog the next morning the *Bear*'s lookout spotted a reef within a few yards of the vessel. If the fog had remained for another half-hour, the ship would have foundered on the rocks. Two days after this narrow escape, the revenue steamer sailed into Port Clarence and found itself in the midst of the whaling fleet waiting at anchor for the ice to recede so that they could go north into the Arctic. There were the barks *Orca, Helen Marr, Hunter, Sea Breeze, Sea Ranger, Wanderer, John and Winthrop, Bounding Billow, Bonanza,* and the steam barks *Balaena* and *Tender Jeanie*—all out of San Francisco. The others were from New Bedford, Massachusetts—*Reindeer, Triton, Alice Knowles, Andrew Hicks, Abram Barker, F. A. Barstow,* and *Horatio.*

The officers of the whaling fleet were men of "more than ordinary character and intelligence, typical American seamen of the best type," according to Jackson. "The common sailors [were] made up largely of Portuguese, Italians, South Sea Islanders, and others of inferior grades. Some of them [were] emphatically, hard cases." The whalers operated on a cooperative plan, with the crew receiving a percentage of the profits rather than wages.

The first whaling vessel ventured into the ice-strewn northern waters about 1840 after the whale had been hunted almost out of existence in the South Pacific. The Arctic slaughter of whales reached tremendous proportions between 1840 and 1890, moving Jackson to compare their fate to the destruction of the great buffalo herds. He also wrote in 1890 that "whereas a few years ago [the walrus] were so numerous that their bellowings were heard above the roar of the waves and the grinding and crashing of the ice fields, this year I have cruised for weeks without seeing or hearing one." Conditions had not improved by 1891.

He took advantage of the meeting with the whaling fleet to make inquiries about the seaman who had been rescued by the Siberian Koriaks and discovered that he was the third mate on the *Abram Barker*. Jackson wanted his assistance because of his friendship with the Siberians and his knowledge of their language. But while the man was willing to co-operate, any agreement between them had to wait until the *Abram Barker* returned to San Francisco in the fall.

The two teachers at the next point of call, Cape Prince of Wales, were disappointed when they found that Jackson had not been able to hire a woman to assist them in the school work. While coal and supplies were being unloaded from the *Bear*, the children at the school demonstrated what they had learned the previous year, and the adults staged a canoe race, the winners receiving three pails of ship's biscuits. Healy then called the natives together and gave them a lecture on the effects of alcohol and the importance of supporting the school. He also appointed ten native policemen to help keep order at the Cape and to control truancy. As a badge of office, each appointee was given a uniform cap. The festivities ended with the firing of three rounds from the *Bear's* twenty-pound howitzer, and the splashing of the shells in the distance made a deep impression on the natives.

Healy steamed for Siberia the following day, cruising in the area of East Cape, Indian Point, and Cape Tchaplin. The greatest difficulty in making contact with the herders lay in the fact that Jackson did not have a competent interpreter. The Siberians could not understand why he wanted to buy reindeer, nor was it easy to explain that the animals could survive transportation to Alaska and a change in habitat.

At Holy Cross Bay, strong winds, ice floes, and a heavy fog forced the steamer to lie at anchor for hours at a time. When the weather had finally lifted enough for Healy to venture into the entrance of the bay, his ship barely cleared the sand bar blocking half the channel. The sole result of this effort was that one herder offered to deliver twenty-five animals at the rate of five deer for one rifle or twenty for a whaleboat—but not until the following season. He also promised to speak to other herders and assured Jackson that he could expect to purchase about two hundred head in 1892. While Jackson's anxiety grew over failure to get reindeer, Healy became increasingly concerned about the return of the ice and the heavy fog which continually enshrouded the bay. The ship's crew remained on twenty-four-hour alert, as the vessel was moved from one spot to another to avoid being trapped. In desperation, Jackson agreed to sail further south to Plover Bay in the hope that his visit there in 1891 might now produce some results.

CHAPTER 7

FIRST REINDEER FROM SIBERIA

Each of the trips that Jackson made in the *Bear* took him across the path of some hardy explorer. Time and again some occasion or event called to his mind the experiences of one or another of the men who had cruised the Bering Sea, the Arctic Ocean, or the Pacific. Their exploits reminded him of the hazards he had to face if he were to succeed in his efforts to help the Eskimos. One of the early explorers to whom he referred in his journals was the English sea captain James Cook, who sailed along the Alaskan coast in the latter part of the eighteenth century. Cook Inlet was named for him, and Cook himself gave Cape Prince of Wales its name. He also cruised along the Siberian coast and identified St. Lawrence Bay.

Plover Bay, where the *Bear* was headed after the disappointing visit to Holy Cross Bay, had gotten its name as the result of a search for another famous English explorer, Rear Admiral Sir John Franklin, who had disappeared while seeking a northwest passage from the Atlantic to the Pacific. A vessel named the *Plover*, while looking for Franklin, had wintered there in 1848-49. Meanwhile, the object of their search lay dead in the vicinity of King William's Island, hundreds of miles to the east in northern Canada.

Healy was reluctant to enter Plover Bay because weather

conditions were as bad as at Holy Cross Bay. Finally he took the *Bear* inside, anchoring in one of the many inlets that burrowed into the surrounding mountains. When they dropped anchor, Jackson recognized that the 2,300-foot peak at the upper end of the inlet was the point named for Robert Kennicott, an American engineer who had taken part in the Western Union Telegraph Expedition of 1866. The expedition had been organized after the first failure of the Atlantic cable in the hope of constructing a telegraph line from Western Europe across Siberia to the vicinity of Plover Bay, then up the Siberian coast to connect with a cable under the Bering Strait to Alaska. The remainder of the system was to run overland down the Pacific coast to the States, but the project was abandoned when the Atlantic cable started to function properly. Jackson's tribute to the expedition was that the adventures and sufferings of its members read like the account of a polar expedition.

One of the men was R. J. Bush, who had been stationed at Plover Bay for almost two years. Bush learned many things about the customs of Siberian natives, and the reports he had made of his discoveries were known to Jackson. On one occasion he noticed a group of natives gathered on the slope of Mt. Kennicott and investigated what they were doing. He thought at first they were taking part in a sacrificial ritual, but as he drew nearer, it seemed to him that they were on an outing. Bush asked his interpreter for an explanation. Pointing to an elderly native who was crouched to one side, the interpreter explained that he was blind and that he was about to be killed because the old man's son had died the previous winter and there was no one to take care of him. Bush noted in his report of the incident that it was also the custom to make the person insensible by having him inhale druglike fumes before being stoned, speared, or bled to death.

In recalling Bush's report, Jackson remembered that he had seen only one old person among the thousands of natives he had encountered along the Siberian coast in 1890 and only two elderly people during the 1891 cruise. "It seems to be a very common practise," he wrote, "that when a person has an incurable disease or becomes too old to be of further service in procuring the necessities of life, to kill him."

Bush also reported on the periodic famines that swept the coastal area. He told of his experience with a native who had asked his advice about whether to sacrifice his dogs or his children in an effort to remain alive. His provisions were so low that they would not suffice for both animals and children until he could get reindeer meat from tribes to the north. He needed the dogs to get the supplies; if he killed them to save the children, everyone would die. Bush could only encourage the bewildered man to keep both children and animals as long as possible in the hope that the deermen would come south.

"Occasionally," Jackson commented on Bush's experience, "an instance of this destitution and starvation comes under the eye of an intelligent white man and is given to the world. But these periodic seasons of starvation come and go, and hundreds of human beings starve and die, their fate unheeded and unknown by the great world outside. To the starving native of Siberia, there is always the possibility of the men who own the large herds hearing of their straits and coming to their relief. But, on the Alaska side, there is nothing left to the people but to starve and die. God hasten the day when the efforts now commencing to introduce the domesticated reindeer into Alaska shall be crowned with success and this dying people saved from utter extinction." But as far as the visit to Plover Bay was concerned, nothing was accomplished, and Healy headed for the American mainland after a week of effort.

Driggs came on board the revenue steamer at Point Hope to report on his first year's work. All natives between the ages of five and twenty-one had attended his school. Classes were largest on stormy days when the children did not have to go out on the ice to fish. The coldest temperature recording at Point Hope in 1890 had been thirty-one degrees below zero; inland where the climate was not moderated by the ocean, it had been much colder.

Healy remained at Point Hope only long enough to unload supplies. He then tried to force his way through the thickening ice to Point Barrow, but conditions worsened so quickly that the attempt had to be given up. Supplies for Barrow were put ashore a hundred miles below the school in the hope that Stevenson could come overland and take them north. During this same period Healy received word that an unidentified steamer had sailed north, apparently unaware of the dangerous ice conditions; he went in pursuit of the stranger in order to warn her captain but had to drop anchor when the fog became too thick. A couple of hours later the unknown vessel was discovered working her way south through the ice. She was the Japanese ship *Tsuri Marie* of Tokyo, chartered at Yokahama by an American bridal party for a walrus hunting expedition to the Arctic. The escapade was dropped when the *Tsuri Marie's* skipper realized it would be a foolhardy effort.

Although suffering from another bad cold, Jackson insisted that a further effort be made to get reindeer from Siberia, and this time the trip was worthwhile. He purchased his first animals on August 28 and wrote in his journal that "this is a great event. It has been proven . . . that they can be purchased alive. It is now to be tested how well they bear transportation."

The next few weeks provided a very good test. Healy crossed

the strait to St. Michael to pick up members of a coast and geodetic survey, landed supplies for starving natives on King Island, and then went back to Siberia for additional animals. It was the middle of September before the first group of reindeer were put ashore at Unalaska Island in charge of the manager of the Alaska Commercial Company; another group were landed on Amaknak Island in the care of the United States deputy marshal.

Jackson's account of this history-making event reads as if he were too tired, too drained emotionally to do more than note what he had been able to accomplish. He made no reference to the fact that the animals survived being penned on the *Bear* during extremely bad weather. Perhaps it is understandable when one realizes that bringing the reindeer to an American possession was almost anticlimactic to the rigorous 17,000-mile journey of 1891 that was required to get the animals to Unalaska and Amaknak Island. After he had sold some of his barter goods to mission stations and stored the remainder for the next year's attempt to get reindeer, Jackson went back to the States. Returning to Unalaska in 1892, he was delighted to find that the animals there were in excellent condition. This spurred him to make five trips that season to Siberia and to purchase another one hundred seventy-five animals. The first small herd was landed on the mainland on July 4, 1892, at Port Clarence, inaugurating the work of the Teller Reindeer station. United States Senator Henry M. Teller, of Colorado, had been Secretary of the Interior when Jackson was named general agent for education; he was Jackson's friend and staunch supporter. The opening of the Teller station was the final step in making the reindeer project a reality. Once the animals were put ashore on the mainland, the Eskimos were headed for a new and prosperous era.

However, the sweet was mixed with the bitter. Jackson's joy

at establishing the Teller station was matched by his sorrow over the murder of a Quaker missionary in 1892 and the receipt of an unpleasant report from Leander Stevenson. The Quaker was Charles H. Edwards, who was in charge of the government contract school at Kake, not far from Juneau. The account of the missionary's death in Jackson's papers has a slightly different color when viewed in the light of how others in Alaska saw it, although there is substantial agreement on the general facts.

Edwards became irked when he found that men aboard a sloop anchored off Kake were selling whiskey to the Indians. To make a citizen's arrest, Edwards took a group of Indians aboard the sloop (at night according to contemporary accounts) to overpower the owner, Malcolm Campbell, and his crew. Edwards was fatally shot during the melee; one Indian was shot and presumably drowned when he dived overboard; another Indian escaped unharmed. The account in Jackson's papers is that, while Edwards tried to sail the vessel to the nearest settlement with the aid of two Indians, having sent the others ashore, Campbell broke loose and shot the missionary and the Indian. In any event, Campbell sailed to Sitka, one hundred and forty miles away, giving rise to the belief among Jackson's friends that he made no effort to save Edwards, who died either just before the sloop reached Sitka or after he was taken ashore—depending on which version one accepts. Either way, the affair ended tragically for the missionary.

According to John Brady, Campbell admitted the shooting but claimed Edwards was committing piracy, the implication being that Campbell had shot in self-defense. Campbell pleaded guilty to the whiskey charge, paid a fine and served a brief jail sentence. An investigation of the shooting resulted in evidence being presented to a grand jury which did not indict Campbell for murder.

This refusal is explained as being due to a number of factors. Indians were believed to have murdered the crews of two small trading vessels and there were other Indian depredations against the whites. Many Indians refused to trade unless it was for whiskey and the general opinion was that Indians got liquor because they wanted it and not because it was forced on them. Others, like Jackson, felt this was a form of casuistry that did not place the initial responsibility for trading in whiskey where it belonged: on the white man. The result was an impasse which was not helped by the values which each side attached to the Edwards' incident.

Some months later, an investigation of the Edwards' affair was made by Allan H. Dougall, an examiner for the United States Attorney General. His findings would leave little doubt that Edwards was murdered in cold blood while trying to uphold the law and that the charges of piracy and of immorality were false. Another probe was made at Kake by a United States deputy marshal, Harry Bourwine; he concluded that Edwards had acted within his rights in trying to make a citizen's arrest. As a sequel, Dr. J. E. Counett, a physician who taught at a government school at Juneau, was tarred and feathered by a group calling itself the Vanguards of Civilization in retaliation for his efforts to get publicity for the Edwards' murder. Dougall identified the leader of the Vanguards as an assistant United States attorney in Alaska, but nothing was ever done to apprehend and try Counett's assailants, just as nothing ever came of the various investigations made into Edwards' death.

Dougall once asked Jackson why it was that "men with stubborn backbones [could not] be selected for official positions in Alaska," then answered his own question in the same letter by pointing out that too much money was involved. He distinguished between two groups of white people in the territory. One consisted of the producers, the men who ran the mines and the fisheries; they favored strict enforcement of the prohibition law because it meant they could then be assured of reliable labor. The other group he classified as the nonproducers, those who preyed on whites and natives and profited from the sale of liquor. Like many persons before and after him, Dougall believed that a federal liquor licensing system would be more effective than prohibition as a means of controlling the whiskey traffic. Jackson, however, never agreed with this point of view. He was committed to groups in the States who stood for total abstinence. Furthermore, a license system had the earmarks of compromise and would still have permitted the natives to get liquor. He was not prepared to accept the lesser of two evils, although under prohibition, bottled goods flowed into Alaska in large quantities from Canada, some of it labeled as Florida Water, Bay Rum, Pain Killer, Jamaica Ginger, and Lemon Extract. One name was as good as another.

Perhaps it was the fact that the whiskey problem was only a symptom of the gross state of neglect under which Alaska languished for years that made Jackson so determined to keep prohibition on the books. But he certainly should have realized that in the face of ineffective law enforcement—even the absence of means to enforce the law—prohibition never stood a chance. Many Alaskans who understood the basic situation quite well tried for years to get Congress to improve the state of affairs in the territory. A nonpartisan convention in 1881 sent a representative to Washington to press for reform, but the mission was doomed before it got under way. A second nonpartisan group met in 1890, elected another representative, and gave him specific instructions. He was to press for improvement in "distorted" jurisprudence, for correction of the faulty judicial system, for a voice for the territory before Congress, for opportunity for Alaskans to get title to land,

and for a voice in the school system. Nothing came of the effort.

One of the barriers to reform in Alaska was the selfishness of the business interests that controlled the economic life of the possession—a combination of American, Canadian, European, and Alaskan financial groups. These interests preferred no legislation to any that might limit their monopolies, regardless of the good intentions that might lie behind reform.

In addition to the Edwards' murder, Jackson's concern for the welfare of Alaska's natives in 1892 was deepened by the report of Leander Stevenson on conditions at Point Barrow. One part detailed Stevenson's experiences with the superintendent of the government refuge station there. Their relationship had so deteriorated that the superintendent was charging him with insubordination, inciting the Eskimos against the whaling seamen, and manufacturing whiskey. Jackson branded the charges as false and malicious. The other part of the report contained Stevenson's opinion of whaling activities and the mistreatment of Eskimos by some whaling men. It is a lurid and emotional account, and one cannot be certain whether Stevenson was describing actual events or reporting what he believed to be true. The teacher felt that many whalers who came to Barrow "never either try or desire to catch a whale, unless one of the great monsters shall try to board them." He claimed that some of these men remained at Barrow, waiting for their ships to return from the east while they had their fill of "squaw hunting." Stevenson was particularly bitter about the fact that Eskimo children were subjected to abuse by some white men. "So lost are the men to every true principle of life . . . and even sense of shame and all those feelings of humanity that prompt to the protection of the weak and defenseless, that they do not hesitate a moment to stultify with liquor or narcotics children not more than ten years of age, force sexual intercourse, keep them in a state of semi-consciousness during their stay, turn them ashore more dead than alive. . . . Add to [this] the many injuries of fraud and theft, with minor outrages, and you have the picture. . . ."

There is no question that the Eskimos received better treatment at the hands of many white people than this described by Stevenson. Jackson himself was high in his praise of the caliber of leadership among officers of the whaling fleet. Just as there would be exceptions among any group of men, Stevenson probably had some basis in fact for his allegations. Jackson, at any rate, thought so, for he had enough corroborative evidence from other areas to know that the lot of the natives was a difficult one at best. Under such circumstances it is easy to understand why he had little sympathy for those who broke the law, and understood no law beyond that of his own Christian convictions.

The truth of the matter is that he was extremely sensitive to certain facts of life as he had observed them in Alaska. This responsiveness led him to the conclusion—as well it might—that Christian ethics as he understood them had to be applied to the assorted ills of the territory. It is to be regretted that being a Christian was equated in Jackson's mind with being a good official; or, to put it another way, that his support of this view earned him much opposition in Alaska while bringing him acclaim in the States. He was probably the author of a memorial addressed to President Harrison by the Presbytery of Alaska on the subject of Christians and Alaskan officials: the belief that "Christian men in office who will both enforce the law and also use their personal influence in favor of sobriety and chastity [are needed]. While there are many honorable men who are not connected with our Christian Churches, yet from our standpoint, we firmly believe that a

President will be less likely to be deceived or make a mistake in the character of his appointments, if for this district he choose Christian men. . . . Eight-tenths of our population are just emerging from barbarism. Like all barbarous races, these people are quick to imitate the vices and slow to adopt the virtues of the whites. And yet those people are simple, teachable, and easily led toward civilization on the one hand, or on the other, as easily led into intemperance and destroyed by the white man's diseases according to the character of the civil officials and their treatment of the people."

This was stating the case fairly, but it came from a group that was looked upon by many Alaskans as meddlers, do-gooders, and pious unrealists too inflexible in their approach to the frontier life of Alaska. But Jackson had an unending succession of reasons for his adamancy, and if he had to reverse his opinion of a man, he was prepared to be forthright in doing so—as in the case of Max Pracht, collector of customs in Alaska. Early in 1890 he wrote to President Harrison charging Pracht with having sold liquor to whites and natives prior to his being appointed collector of customs and with appointing deputy collectors who were often under the influence of whiskey. He offered evidence that Pracht had used various stratagems to bring contraband into the territory and concluded the affidavit by saying that "in the eleven or twelve years I have been acquainted with southeast Alaska, I have never known so much drunkenness and demoralization from liquor." A year later, Jackson was still importuning President Harrison to remove Pracht from office and at the same time asking that he, Jackson, be protected from recrimination:

"The contents of the letter I sent you last spring concerning Mr. Pracht was sent him, and has brought me more or less persecution. . . . Now I have not lost faith in your earnest desire to give Alaska good officials, but you have been woefully deceived by politicians urging these men upon you. . . . I have no interest in this matter other than that of good government, and the good name of your administration. In God's good providence, you and a portion of your excellent cabinet are Presbyterians. This has given rise to the term Presbyterian Administration, and it is the constant taunt that Alaska missionaries are called to bear, as the godless point to the Collector, the Judge, and other officials, and say 'see your good Presbyterian officials.' The Lord give you wisdom for your difficult and trying place."

CHAPTER 8

SHIPWRECK IN THE ARCTIC

Of all the predicaments Jackson had to face, the easiest to overcome were the premature reports of his death. Some of his friends believed that they were the result of wishful thinking. He himself paid little attention to them, for the fact of his existence was substantial evidence of the inappropriateness of the obsequies. The first account of the end of his career was carried in a wire service story out of Victoria, British Columbia, dated March 15, 1892:

"Intelligence has been received here of the drowning in the Skirma River, Alaska, of Reverend Mr. Sheldon, Mrs. Cunningham, and two Indians. It is thought the minister referred to is Reverend Sheldon Jackson, the noted Indian missionary, in charge of the Indian schools of Alaska under the direction of the government."

It is likely that the death of the Quaker missionary Charles Edwards was the basis of this story, especially because of the reference to the two Indians. Reports of Jackson's death were still making the rounds in June 1892; one friend wrote to him, "I expect to find you alive notwithstanding the newspaper reports of your recent murder by Yukon Indians. It is not a common occurrence for a man to read his obituary so frequently. . . ."

One of the persons who were anxious to get confirmation

or denial of Jackson's death was his friend of long standing Miss Frances A. Willard, the president of the National Woman's Christian Temperance Union, the World's Woman's Christian Temperance Union, and the very influential Woman's National Council. The reply to Miss Willard's inquiry, which had been directed to a close friend of the Jackson family, is interesting for the characterization it offers of the man:

"Dear Miss Willard,

"I received this very morning an hour before your letter arrived a pleasant communication from Dr. Sheldon Jackson's daughter, thanking me for the only *cheery* letter among hundreds [all of condolence]. We who knew how anxious the papers are for news of Alaska, understood instantly this was a canard founded on the fact of a missionary who was killed last winter trying to arrest smugglers and revised to suit. [Dr. Jackson] is a thoroughgoing, practical, earnest, business agent for the Board of Missions. . . . He is a born politician and has made more enemies than any other man, missionary or otherwise, who has ever visited Alaska or any other territory. He is indefatigable and even his enemies give him credit for never swerving. They call him a buzz saw, saying he cuts both ways to accomplish [his] ambition. . . ."

There is more than a grain of truth in the letter, although it is a question whether Jackson was a politician in the sense in which that word is usually understood. But there can be no argument with the assertion—even though it was made with righteous indignation—that he made more enemies in Alaska than anyone else.

The year 1893 produced the first tangible reaction in Congress to the reindeer project when six thousand dollars was appropriated for the work. This came about, in part, as a result of the experience at Teller Station. The animals landed in 1892 produced seventy-nine fawn and even though twenty-nine died, there were two hundred and twenty healthy specimens when Jackson arrived in 1893. However, there was one disturbing matter at the station. Bruce Miner, the newly appointed superintendent, was charged by Captain Healy with selling rifles to the natives, and his discharge was requested. It was probably this incident that prompted Jackson to send a letter to all personnel under his supervision:

"I am informed some missionaries and teachers in Western Alaska have traded breech-loading firearms and cartridges to the natives. . . . I trust this is a mistake. Missionaries and government teachers, of all others, should set an example of observing the law. The statement, however, had been so confidently made that I feel it but proper to officially notify all stations that the selling, trading, or giving away of cartridges and guns will be considered a sufficient cause for the immediate dismissal of the offender. . . ."

Miner was replaced by Lopp, from Cape Prince of Wales, but he had to return to his former work when the man who succeeded him was murdered by natives. The man who finally took over the Teller assignment was William Kjelmann, of Madison, Nebraska. Jackson could not have asked for a more loyal and dedicated co-worker.

In the midst of the dispute over Miner's activities, there was another situation that needed correction. The original plan had been to hire Siberians to take care of the reindeer in Alaska because they were the only persons available. But the Siberians did a poor job, allowing the herds to split into small groups and mix with passing caribou, with the result that some of the imported animals reverted to their normal wild state. Even more seriously, however, the Siberians were careless with the newborn fawn and many of the young died. Jackson decided that if the project was not to suffer he would have to find competent herders. As a result, he sent Kjelmann to Lapland in an emergency effort to persuade a small group of Laplanders to come and work with the animals and train Alaskan natives to handle them. There were no funds to defray the cost of the trip, so Jackson appealed to friends, who contributed one thousand dollars. Kjelmann returned to Teller in two months with seven Lapps and their families, sixteen persons in all. The wisdom in the effort was clear at once. The Lapps knew their business and made excellent instructors. Whereas the Siberians had lost forty-nine fawn out of one hundred and eighty-six in one season, only three fawn were lost out of two hundred and fifteen births during the first year that the Lapps were in charge.

As always, Jackson had to face unpleasant news even while enjoying events favorable to his work, and 1893 was no exception. With the reindeer in good hands, he heard from Captain Healy that the captain of an American vessel had gone to Siberia and traded whiskey for reindeer. The result was that the Siberians had lost interest in trading their stock for pots and pans. To make matters worse, they realized that they had something which the Americans wanted. Past purchase agreements went by the board, prices were raised to exorbitant levels, and instead of being able to buy two hundred and fifty animals during the 1893 season, Jackson had to be satisfied with one hundred and twenty-seven. Eventually, the Teller herd contributed its bit by increasing its own size to three hundred and seven head by the end of 1893.

There was also a renewal of school administration difficulties in 1893. Lyman Knapp, the governor who succeeded Swineford, charged that Jackson was neglecting his responsibilities. In turn, Knapp was charged with having made his complaint without any personal knowledge of the school system. People in Sitka said that he had not visited their school for white children and had only the vaguest contact with schools in nearby settlements; therefore, he had no basis upon which to charge Jackson with dereliction of duty. Even so, the Knapp charge kept the fire of opposition smouldering, although the Office of Education in Washington did not take the complaint seriously. It was about this same time that Jackson had the temerity to propose that Congress raise the annual school appropriation to seventy-five thousand dollars, and he wrote to a number of congressmen and senators asking them to support the increase. Senator P. B. Plumb replied in a manner that reflected the level of the opposition:

"My opinion is that a considerable portion of the money which has been spent for education in Alaska has been misspent. It has enabled some people to live very comfortably in the states, to spend most of their time away from the proper theatre of their work, to pose as philanthropists, and so on, and has brought little or no good to the Indians of Alaska. For these reasons I do not . . . favor an increase in the appropriation already existing."

While Jackson was being charged with incompetency, dishonesty, and self-indulgence, there were ample facts to show that he had performed well as general agent for education. Seventeen government schools were in operation in Alaska at the start of 1893, barely eight years after he had received his appointment. There were two schools at Sitka, at Juneau, and at Douglas (including schools for whites only). There were single schools located at Jackson, Wrangell, Chilcat, Kodiak, Afognak, Karluk, and Unga. Part-time schools were in operation at Kake, Klawock, Killisnoo and Port Clarence. Seven hundred and forty-five pupils attended these schools at an estimated cost to the federal government of twenty thousand dollars a year.

There were, in addition, fourteen schools associated with

mission stations, called contract operations. They were sponsored by the Presbyterians at Sitka, Hoonah, and Point Barrow; by the Roman Catholics at Holy Cross, Nulato, and Cape Vancouver; by the Episcopalians at Point Hope and Anvik; by the Moravians at Bethel and Carmel; by the Methodists at Unalaska; by the Congregationalists at Cape Prince of Wales; by the Swedish Evangelical Mission at Yakutat; and at Metlakatla under Father Duncan. At the start of 1893, one thousand one hundred and two students were enrolled in these schools at a cost to the government of thirty thousand dollars. The average cost per pupil for both government and contract schools was twenty-seven dollars a year. Another two hundred and ninety-two pupils were studying industrial arts at mission-operated institutions supported by individual denominations entirely without federal assistance. The Presbyterian industrial training school at Sitka was the largest of these. Furthermore, all church-related schools were open the year-round, which was not true of some government schools.

Jackson's very important contribution to Alaska's school system was his ability to interest missionary organizations in making vital financial contributions. American denominations spent about eighty thousand dollars a year on teachers' salaries and improvements to school properties at their missions. This was above the annual federal appropriation of fifty thousand dollars. While the missionary zeal of the churches was such that they would have sustained the schools without aid from the state, their participation with Jackson's encouragement added immeasurably to the effectiveness of the system as a whole. The truth is that the churches underwrote a disproportionate share of the school costs. The Presbyterians, for example, operated six missions in the 1890's, with schools attached valued at ninety-five thousand dollars. They paid the expenses of thirty-seven teachers and employees, clothed and boarded two hundred and fourteen children, and cared for another two hundred day pupils. Other denominations participated in the support of Alaska's schools to the best of their ability. Jackson knew better than anyone else that it was only with the greatest amount of sacrifice that the various denominations continued their educational work and that the federal government was falling far short of what it should have been doing. He felt he needed at least sixty thousand dollars a year as demands for schools and improvements mounted month by month. Seventy-five thousand dollars would have given him greater leeway. Meanwhile Senator Plumb and others proposed that the existing fifty thousand annual appropriation be reduced to forty thousand.

Alaska's school population was between eight and ten thousand in 1893, but there were facilities for only two thousand students. Efforts to improve the status of the natives had resulted in a sharp reduction in the mortality rate among children, which in turn was reflected in the rising native school age population. As demands for new facilities increased, costs also rose. With Congress' refusal to provide means for raising funds locally, all monies for school purpose had to come from Washington. Jackson reported that he had kept the school system functioning at its 1893 level by means of stringent economies at points where it did the most harm—the teachers' salaries. He warned that a forty thousand dollar appropriation would require further cutbacks and the hiring of less competent teachers because they would be the only ones who would accept lower wages.

Again he underscored the disgraceful attitude of Congress by pointing out that the seal island leases had poured nine million dollars into the federal treasury in twenty years, with an estimated fifteen million more for the next twenty-year lease. To make matters worse, the lack of regard for the educational needs of the natives was backfiring against the whites.

The man who succeeded Lyman Knapp as governor of Alaska, James Sheakley, strongly supported Jackson's efforts on behalf of the schools throughout his tenure of office, 1893-1897. For six years before his appointment as governor, Sheakley had been a United States Commissioner in Alaska; he was, therefore, able to urge improvements in the school system out of a knowledge of the actual needs. He backed Jackson's insistence that local school committees were a mistake. Few people, he felt, were qualified to sit on such committees, and those who were willing usually had some selfish motive. Supporting instead the proposal for dividing the territory into three major school districts, he suggested that someone be appointed to administer the schools in the southeast. "You know it takes a great deal of time and labor to manage these schools properly," he wrote to Jackson. Furthermore, he was satisfied that the school funds were being spent judiciously. But nothing could be done to alter Congress' attitude. In 1895, when there were twenty-nine government schools, Sheakley tried to get more funds so that all schools could be supplied with teachers. He got nowhere.

It was inevitable that the shortage of funds should produce certain lesions in the school system and effect its operation. The curriculum, for instance, was not all it should have been, resulting in part from the fact that not all teachers could handle all subjects.

When all this is understood, it becomes fairly clear that many of the complaints over the operation of the schools in Alaska were directed more at making Jackson the scapegoat than in getting Congress to improve the situation.

Jackson's annual inspection trip of Alaskan schools in 1894 did not have an auspicious beginning. The *Bear* left Port

Townsend, Washington, on May 5 and headed out the Strait of Juan de Fuca during one of the worst storms in years. Off Cape Flattery, the wind churned the ocean into a nightmare, driving sheets of sleet and rain across the vessel. The sleet turned into snow and the wind developed gale force. The *Bear*'s forestaysail was torn to shreds. The after-wheel ropes became unhooked. A yardarm snapped and crashed through the wheelhouse, but no one was harmed. On the fifth day one of the ship's cutters was carried away while tons of water poured below decks and rose knee-deep in the galley. The snow then became a torrential downpour, changing again to a blinding snowstorm. With the furious pitch and toss of the steamer no one was able to get any rest. Jackson himself became violently ill. When after several days he was finally able to keep food down, he had to stand in the pilothouse eating out of his hands like an animal. By the time the *Bear* reached Sitka on May 11, eight inches of snow was blanketing the town. Farther north the steamer ran into other troubles because of the lack of up-to-date charts. Those available were off at many points; using them was as hazardous as ignoring them altogether. This was just one more result of Congress' inaction, which seafarers had come to accept as an inevitable part of life in Alaska.

During this trip Jackson visited two settlements sharply in contrast with one another and demonstrated what could be done for the natives. The first was located in Cordova Bay. It consisted of twenty-five white men, twenty-five native women, and twenty-five stills capable of producing twenty-five hundred gallons of liquor, mostly consumed by natives. They had no other visible means of support, although during the canning season the men did catch fish. He identified the other as Nilchik, to the southwest. There, one American and seventeen native families were living, totaling fifty-three healthy persons, including twenty-three children between six and twenty-one. The homes of the natives were small but well kept. Most of the families had vegetables; a few even had several head of cattle.

He visited a third settlement at Kenai, on Cook Inlet. Here the entire population of one hundred and fifty were suffering from the effects of grippe which had swept the settlement four years earlier. Forty persons had already died, and the survivors were left in such weakened condition that their prospects of surviving new illnesses were very low.

The situation Jackson found at Kodiak was a repetition of that which he had encountered elsewhere in trying to get the support of local Russian Orthodox priests. The Baptist missionaries at Kodiak complained that the local priest was hampering their efforts to help the diseased, dirty, and hungry orphans in the town. On one occasion, when the missionaries had taken a boy into their home and were well on the way to rehabilitating him, the priest got a court order for the child's release. However, instead of helping the boy, the priest allowed him to return to his former ways; hence when Jackson was in Kodiak, the child was in as bad a shape as he had been the day the missionaries had taken him off the street. The opposition of the Orthodox priests had also been reported to Jackson by Moravian mission stations. Therefore, though he was prepared for what he heard at Kodiak, it added another burden to his heart.

The *Bear* continued its westward cruise in the direction of Sitkalidak Island, which guarded the entrance to Three Saints Bay. The island was the site of the first permanent Russian settlement in Alaska, dating back to 1784. The first school was built there by the Russians in 1785 and the first church in the territory in 1796. Unfortunately, from then up to the time of Jackson's arrival in 1894, little or no progress had been made in either education or religion. If anything, both had declined since the Americans had taken over.

As the vessel sailed through the North Pacific headed for Unga, it passed close to Chirikof Island, which Jackson described as the Botany Bay of Russian America. For years it had served as a penal colony for the more desperate criminals with whom the Russians had tried to colonize the Aleutians. As their number increased, the Russians allowed Chirikof to fend for itself, and it became self-supporting—so much so that when the United States bought Alaska, no one on the island was informed of the fact. It was not until 1869 when Vincent Colyer, the United States Indian Commissioner, visited Chirikof on a tour of inspection, that the island's inhabitants discovered they no longer had to fear the Russian knout. The entire colony promptly took off for Kodiak, eighty miles away, and became "lost" in their new-found freedom.

After the stop at Unga, Healy headed for Unalaska to take part in an unexpected drama of the North Pacific which had started while the *Bear* was battling her way up the southeast coast earlier in the season. A storm far worse than that encountered by the revenue steamer was raging hundreds of miles to the west along the tip of the Aleutians. Here the whaling bark *James Allen*, while trying to navigate dangerous Saguam Pass into the Bering Sea, piled up on a reef and was doomed at once. Captain Arthur Huntly gave orders to abandon ship and took off himself in the last of the five cutters. As his cutter was being lowered, it smashed against the side of the *Allen*. The crew were forced to pull furiously at the oars and leave the bailing to later, for the *Allen* turned turtle and sank stern first. As soon as they were at a safe distance, Huntly concentrated on keeping the cutter afloat. The storm drove his boat eastward in the direction of Amlia Island. Three hours later, just as day broke, he went aground on the island

and discovered that two other boats had gone ashore at the same point. There was no sign of the remaining cutters. Not until a month later was it known that the men in one of the missing boats had been saved, but the others were lost.

The task of surviving on Amlia drove concern for the fate of the other seamen from everyone's mind. For two days while the storm continued, they huddled in the lee of rock ledges, living on seaweed, mussles, and a few cod caught with hooks made out of bailing wire. The storm abated sufficiently on the third day to risk an attempt to get out past the breakers and make for Unalaska, two hundred and forty miles away. They used one of the boats, rigged out with a sail made of bed quilts, to tow the other two. But a new storm threatened to sink the lead boat because its stern dragged low in the water under the pressure of the towline. Therefore, the three cutters separated, each to the mercy of the gale, which drove all of them along the same course to the Islands of the Four Mountains. The seas were running so high here that to try to reach shore would have been suicide. Instead the cutters were anchored to patches of heaving, offshore kelp to keep them from being blown to sea and certain destruction. The men were too numb with cold and fear to go farther; they could do nothing but lie crouched in the boats throughout the night in constant dread of being torn loose from their moorings.

The next morning when they got to shore, they found water but no food. They had the choice of staying on the island at the risk of starving to death before help might arrive, or taking the equally big risk of putting back to sea and running the gauntlet of the bad weather. Huntly made his choice when one of the seamen died shortly after the landing. He left one leaking cutter behind and divided the strongest of the men between the remaining two. By mid-afternoon, Huntly's boat had capsized opposite Umnak Island. Four of his men were drowned, weighted down by the heavy clothing they wore to protect them from the storm. The survivors were hauled into the remaining boat, by then so overloaded with its twenty-one passengers that it was in constant danger of going under. Huntly put in to shore at once on the eastern end of Umnak, the seamen scrambling over the side in their haste to reach safety. Some fell face down in the surf and had to be dragged to the beach. Another died the following day. As the captain watched the mark of death creep across the faces of the rest, he realized that he had to make an effort to reach Unalaska if any were to come through alive. With the six ablest, he tried to launch the cutter; but the heavy surf balked every effort, once almost capsizing the boat.

Two more died the next day. When someone found a deserted hunter's shack, they were able to get out of the bad weather. Huntly made new efforts to get off the island during the course of the next few days, but each time he was thwarted by the danger of wrecking the cutter in the surf. It was not until June 5—the same day that the *Bear*, with Jackson aboard, reached Chirikof Island far to the east—that the captain got away from Umnak. On that day too, another of the *Allen*'s seamen died.

Neither the men Huntly took with him nor those he left behind on Umnak had much hope that they would see one another again or even that they would survive. Those who went with the captain, spurred by a slim chance of reaching Unalaska alive, spent what little strength they had during the first day and a half. The rest of the time they were too weak and discouraged to do more than allow the cutter to drift with the wind and the tide. Night passed overhead and the ocean surged below for almost a week. On the seventh day, Huntly thought that he recognized the entrance to Unalaska harbor, but he was unwilling to believe his eyes for fear that they were betraying him. He slumped in the stern, not daring to lose sight of the headland but certain that it would turn out to be a false hope. Only when the cutter was at the harbor entrance did he dare to arouse the men with him. Nothing but a hoarse sound left his puffed, cracked lips, but it was enough to attract the attention of one sailor who, turning his head, simply stared at the shore without making a sound. Another turned to look and then slumped over the side of the boat.

The *Bear* was in Unalaska at the time undergoing minor engine repairs. One of her crew spotted the cutter and sounded the alarm. A small boat entering the harbor could only mean that disaster had befallen a ship somewhere in the North Pacific. Survivors were taken on board the revenue steamer for first aid. Then as soon as Healy had heard Huntly's story, he gave orders for the *Bear* to prepare to get under way in four hours. She put to sea in spite of the fact that a new storm was already upon her. The U.S.S. *Albatross,* which Healy had asked to accompany the *Bear* in the event of further trouble, was unable to clear the harbor entrance because the weather worsened so quickly. Once outside the protection of the anchorage, the *Bear* was buffeted so severely by the storm that she was unable to do more than two knots an hour under full steam. Not until the following afternoon did she reach Umnak Island, and then Healy had to remain offshore for another twenty-four hours before he could risk landing a rescue party. Huntly, who had insisted on returning to the island, commanded one of the *Bear*'s cutters. He was the first person to reach the beach and ran straight for the hut where he had last seen his men. But when he came in sight of the place, he was dumbstruck by what he saw. The men were alive—at least it seemed most of them were—but they bore little resemblance to the crew he had commanded.

They were crouching around a fire, over which a small pot hung suspended, their dirty, bearded, emaciated faces fixed upon it with animal-like intensity. Somehow they had found something to eat. Huntly could not imagine what it was, nor was he anxious to find out. He could hear them grunting in loathsome expectation of the coming meal. Without waiting to see or hear anything more, he ran up to them, calling out as he ran. For a while they just sat on their haunches and stared at him, not able to comprehend what was happening. Then the truth sank home and they fell back in a state of complete exhaustion. On board the *Bear* after they had been treated by the ship's surgeon, they told the story of the fire and the pot in halting, anguished apology. The day following Huntly's departure they had decided that they would never see him again, and like animals they could think only of how to remain alive as long as possible. Two of them had died the day after Huntly left; the rest turned to cannibalism.

The horrible irony of it was that all that time they had been only six miles from an Aleut village on the other side of the island. Healy took them to Dutch Harbor, where they arrived one month and six days after the *Allen* had gone down, and transferred them to a vessel headed for San Francisco. Jackson transcribed Huntly's entire account of the episode, adding details which he himself had witnessed. All in all, it brought him closer than he had even been before to the cruelness of the Arctic.

Having completed her rescue mission, the *Bear* went back to Unalaska so that Jackson could continue his efforts to find a suitable site on which to build a new school. The day after their arrival, word was received that there were shipwrecked sailors on Saguam Island, in the same area where the *Allen* had sunk. Everyone thought that the report had stemmed from the wreck of the whaler, but in order to make certain

Healy left Unalaska, searched the waters around Saguam, and checked the island for signs of shipwreck. Finding nothing he concluded that the story had come either from the wreck of the *Allen* herself or as a result of the rescue of the men in her fourth cutter, which had been found drifting off Atka Island by an employee of the Alaska Commercial Company.

When the search of the Saguam area was completed, Healy headed for Siberia and Cape Navarin. The bold and rugged coast stretching north and south of the point loomed through the clearing fog on June 27. But there was no other reason for rejoicing because none of the natives who had promised to deliver animals were on hand. He sailed down the coast, still without success, until squally weather forced him to put in at Plover Bay. Two days later, after performing a small mission on St. Lawrence Island in American waters, the *Bear* was back off the Siberian coast. This time she found two herders awaiting her arrival. After hours of negotiation, forty-eight animals were traded and ferried out to the steamer.

Always on the verge of being caught in the ice, Healy spent the next ten days moving up and down the coast in the hope of finding other natives willing to sell. Some were sighted on several occasions, but each time the revenue ship had to be taken out to sea when the wind drove heavy ice floes toward land. At other times, when the *Bear* could remain close to shore, the deermen refused to deliver animals for which they had been paid. Then the inevitable caught up with Healy; a sudden shift in the wind trapped the steamer in a mass of ice from which there was no escape. In a desperate effort to break loose, he worked the vessel back and forth until one of her propellers was broken, and the disaster that was always imminent seemed to have her in its clutches. But the wind shifted again, and the *Bear* drifted clear of the ice mass into open water where the crew was able to replace the propeller. The same trouble occurred the following day and another propeller was broken. Once again the wind changed, freeing the steamer of the ice, but this time Healy decided he had had enough and headed back to American waters. The reindeer were landed at Teller Station on July 25. Because of Jackson's other responsibilities in connection with the schools, that was the last trip to Siberia during the 1894 season.

In making his rounds of the schools, Jackson stopped off at Point Hope to leave mail and supplies and to check requirements for the coming year. John Driggs, the teacher in charge of that post, came on board the *Bear* to make his report. The doctor showed signs of the strain of living in a sterile region which offered nothing to a white man but the daily struggle against loneliness, days without sunlight, and the never-ending assault of the weather. Driggs had the added responsibility of breaking through the wall of superstition that separated him from the natives who needed his medical skill. There were weeks when he felt defeated in every effort to combat the potions and rituals with which the native medicine men tried to effect cures. When it was almost too late for help, they brought him their sick, thereby increasing the odds against him in his struggle to overcome the influence of their shamans. Even when the natives seemed to respond to his efforts, Driggs found evidence that they were far from being free of the habits of centuries.

He was out walking one day when he met an Eskimo whom he had treated several months previously. The man was overjoyed at seeing the doctor and explained, as best he could, that his head and chest hurt him no longer. Driggs was pleased. He urged the man to tell his friends how the white doctor had helped him. Then the the native pulled from his pocket the medicine Driggs had given him, to show that he was taking good care of the white man's magic—a convert from the potions of the native medicine men to the witchcraft of the American doctor. On another occasion Driggs came upon a native funeral procession for a man whom he had tried to cure. Another setback to be overcome, he thought. When the wife of the dead man caught sight of the doctor, she insisted that he look at her husband's body. She pulled back the cover and, to Driggs' surprise, showed him the bottle of medicine he had given the man, firmly clutched in his lifeless hands. The widow explained that she had put it there because she believed it would most certainly be of help to her husband wherever he was going.

Driggs also described to Jackson the epidemic that hit Point Hope in the summer of 1893 when capillary bronchitis swept through the native village and took the lives of one out of every six persons. Three quarters of the Eskimos were seriously ill at one time despite every effort to check the disease. Often there were not enough well people to bury the dead; they had to be left in the street, a prey for the dogs.

Point Hope was just one of many places in Alaska where the larger struggle for survival had to be waged without end. Men like Jackson, whose devotion to the land and its people stemmed from humanitarian and spiritual impulses, were painfully aware of the need for stinging Congress out of its indifference, indeed for making the entire nation aware of the tragedies that stalked unchecked across the territory from one end to the other, days without end. They felt too as if they were working on an oft-mended garment in their struggle to relieve Alaska's ills. No sooner were they able to repair one spot than another gave way, but they continued to work in the hope that a new and worthy replacement could be found to shield her bruised body before the old garment fell into shreds.

While prospects were improving for the Eskimos, the Indians and the whites in the southeast needed help in preserving one of Alaska's great natural resources—fish. Commercial interests had caught salmon for years with no regard for the destruction wrought by their greedy and illegal methods. When Alaskans induced Congress to pass legislation that forbade certain fishing practices, there were too few inspectors to make certain that the laws were enforced. The depletion of the salmon was an even greater blow to the Indians, who depended on their fish catch for a large part of their food. Many whites were more concerned with getting Congress to impose a tax on each can of salmon as a means of providing revenue for the development of local communities and the expansion of the school system, but some also recognized the more basic danger.

The commercial fisheries, of course, were not too interested in complying with the regulations enacted by Congress. To the tax they were completely opposed, arguing that it was unfair to them. If there was any unfairness in the situation, it affected the territory's future. It was not as if every locality in Alaska was a wretched conglomeration of frontier life, satisfied with a makeshift existence, without pride or hope for the future. Many communities had developed amazingly well in spite of their handicaps, but left without sources of income, their future was uncertain. Juneau, to cite but one example, had a population of about two thousand persons late in the 1890's, about one third being white. There were nine general stores doing a thriving business, three hotels or lodging houses, drug and hardware stores, a photographic studio, a steam laundry, a millinery shop, three schools, churches, a hospital, a theatre of sorts, newspapers, paved streets, and organized fire protection. The harbor was good but in need of improved facilities. The fact is that the town compared favorably with many of like size in the American West; but compared to them, Juneau led a stepchild's existence.

For a brief period Alaskans were in hope that Congress

would pass the salmon tax and enact effective controls over the fishing industry, but they reckoned without the pressures brought to bear by vested interests. When the 1895-97 session eventually passed an Alaskan omnibus bill, Alaskans found out that the salmon tax had been dropped, and no adequate means had been provided for enforcing the few fishing regulations. One of the federal fish industry inspectors, L. N. Ketcham, complained bitterly in a letter to Jackson about the conditions under which he was supposed to do a good job. He had the choice of covering the great distances in his area by canoe and arriving at his destinations long after the salmon catch was ended, or accepting passage on a cannery company boat with resultant obligations to the company. He was understandably resentful of the treatment he received aboard one of the vessels of the Pacific Coast Steamship Company, which had a monopoly of Alaska's communication with the States. He reported that he spent his time between an "abominable room and the storage, in both of which places it was impossible to catch any sleep," with the result that he was seldom in physical shape to do his job. Ketcham paid full, first-class fare for his passage and felt that he was entitled to be "as well and as quietly housed as anyone else on the ship," particularly since he was a government officer. But that, in Alaska, was hardly the basis upon which to expect good treatment; federal officials were not held in very high repute, largely because of the activities of the officers themselves.

Ketcham had another concern which he held in common with almost all of Jackson's correspondents—the unfavorable moral climate in Alaska and its genesis, the liquor traffic. He apologized for bringing up the subject, adding that he realized the general agent was very familiar with it. The greatest handicap to the tremendous job of education remaining to be done, he wrote, was the traffic in liquor. He implored Jackson to make even greater attempts to impress upon the administration in Washington the need for a stronger judiciary and a more effective customs force in the territory:

"I am satisfied," Ketcham wrote, "that on each regular ship there is a gang of operators who deal in contraband whiskey and opium, in quantities comparatively small, it is true, but large enough to be mischievous and dangerous everywhere. There is no principle involved in the traffic; it is simply and wholly a method of making money, and whiskey in bottles upon every opportunity is sold to all comers: reputable white men, white scoundrels who in turn sell to Indians, and direct to Indians themselves."

Ketcham did not believe that the officers of the ships were involved in selling liquor to the Indians or in bringing native women on board for prostitution. But "Indian drunkenness is almost as regular as the ship's visit. And sooner or later it will result in the murder of the whites. . . ."

One interesting point in this analysis is that it follows a pattern that was always clear: responsibility for immorality always belonged to someone other than those who by virtue of their authority and position should have taken a leading role in correcting it. Perhaps Ketcham feared that if he denounced the ships' officers he would have to bear the repercussions and that it was simpler to attack the traffic in liquor and drugs by placing the major onus on underlings. It is difficult to escape the conclusion that the ships' officers could have controlled what took place on board their vessels if they had wanted to do so—assuming that what Ketcham described was accurate. It would appear that, in matters of enforcing the law, everyone's business became no one's business. Too much emphasis cannot be placed upon the state of apathy that developed among Alaskans as they struggled in vain to win their rightful place in the American nation.

As for Ketcham's fears that there would be a bloody Indian uprising, there was never a time when the whites in Alaska had to fear attacks to the degree familiar in the American West. In 1879, Sitkans were sufficiently upset by the possibility of Indian attacks to ask for the protection of a British man-of-war until the arrival of an American warship. Through the years, while Indians in Alaska attacked isolated white men on occasions, there were no large-scale assaults.

Ever since President Chester Arthur had told Congress that he hoped it would "not fail to put Alaska under the protection of the law [for] its people have repeatedly remonstrated against our neglect," successive presidents had voiced the same hope without getting results. There were occasions when even presidential messages ignored the situation in Alaska. The territory did not receive its first taxation and a criminal code designed to meet its particular needs until 1899. Another year passed before Congress voted an improved civil code. If legislative neglect did not produce enough sorrow for Alaskans, the carpetbaggers filled their cup of woe to overflowing. They flocked to Alaska knowing of the vacuum in which they could operate, and they found enough willing tools among those who lived there to infest every place with the amorality and immorality they brought with them. Nichols says it is a wonder that Alaska did not suffer even more from carpetbaggers. She feels that all that saved the territory was the fact that most of the higher officials "had something of the good brought out in them through contact wih the more sturdy class of pioneers. Nevertheless, the popular wrath vented itself upon Alaskans as often as upon carpetbaggers, upon honest officials as well as upon scoundrels."

Quite likely Alaskans reached the stage where they felt themselves incapable of discriminating between good and bad officials, inasmuch as all came from the same source. In this way

Jackson inherited his share of the opprobrium.

As for the first taxation law and criminal code passed by Congress in 1899, its primary purpose was to establish a licensing system to take the place of prohibition. There are no indications, however, that passage of the law decreased the number of saloons in operation in the territory, nor was that the real intention of the tax law. The levy was imposed on all businesses—fisheries, gold mines, boarding houses, and so forth—with 50 per cent of the receipts to be returned to local communities for educational purposes. The civil code which was passed in 1900 provided additional courts at Nome and Eagle. In addition, there were communities where court had been held in the past, such as Wrangell and Juneau. Alaskans could not agree among themselves on the merits of the codes; it is certainly true that they only touched up and did not fully meet the basic needs of the territory.

No place in the world was a better example of the thesis that a house divided against itself cannot stand than Alaska. The sharp division of opinion that existed over the political development of the territory was apparent in the third nonpartisan convention of 1899-1900—nonpartisan in the sense that all shades of opinion were to be represented. The meeting was called by people who lived in Skagway, Juneau, and Douglas. Sitkans refused to attend. They did not relish the thought that Juneau would become the territorial capital, and any meeting that might possibly advance such a proposal was certain to meet with their opposition. The convention went on record with a demand for more schools for white children, but it was primarily called in order to get more home rule for the territory. The question over which the delegates divided was how best to achieve that result. Some preferred an elected delegate to Congress. Others favored the creation of a territorial legislature, believing that only Alaskans could improve the conditions in Alaska and that nothing could be expected from Washington until the territory itself was organized. Supporters of the delegate plan, on the other hand, argued that the presence of a representative in Washington would be sufficient to get Congress to act upon Alaska's needs. With such a basic split in approach, the nonpartisan convention of 1899-1900 produced little or not result. As the years went by and Alaskans saw Puerto Rico, Hawaii, and the Philippines receive the right of representation before Congress, skepticism in the territory spread wider and deeper than before.

In the face of such conditions, it is surprising that Jackson was able to accomplish as much as he did. He might have done more if he had not been involved in so many facets of territorial life and if he had not been linked so closely with Washington officialdom. But that is only wishful thinking. Jackson was what he was. It was clear from the start of his work in Alaska that he would have his hand in every phase of life because everything impinged on what he was attempting to do. He was the right man in the right place at the right time. His mission was prescribed in the providence of God; at least that is how he himself felt about it, and that was sufficient motivation for him.

And Mrs. Jackson—how did she view her husband's sense of mission? With whatever sacrifices were needed to make his triumphs possible! Her early religious training gave her understanding of the importance of his work. She married him knowing the support he would need and she never faltered.

Life in the Jackson home was constantly interrupted by his extended trips into the field. There were weeks—sometimes months—when his wife did not know his exact whereabouts. One of the Jackson children said in later years that she could not remember her father being at home very often. This must have been particularly difficult for Mrs. Jackson when one of her four daughters died in 1861 and several years later an infant died. Mrs. Jackson herself suffered a number of illnesses while her husband was away.

She was even denied that comfort which is important to most women—having one place to call home. She lived for varying periods in Spencer, Oklahoma, La Crescent and Rochester, Minnesota, Council Bluffs, Nebraska, Denver, Colorado, New York City, and Washington, D.C.—as well as intermittent stays at Galesburg, Illinois.

One can only marvel at her endurance and patience.

It would appear that on several occasions when she accompanied him on trips his need of her companionship was the factor that made her go. She was ill before going to Alaska in 1879 and sickness forced her early return to the States when she was with him in Sitka early in 1885. Nor did she look forward to the trip to Arizona to gather a group of Indian children. She confided to a friend that she thought she had seen the last of that desolate area.

On at least one occasion she made it clear that she did not favor a proposal to change her husband's field of work. Following a trip to Texas, she wrote to a churchman there and received this reply: ". . . there has been no connivance with the [board] secretaries to disturb your peace and happiness. . . . Your dread of Texas mosquitoes need not alarm you for they are not everywhere and even the hot weather you would endure under more favorable circumstances than when you were here. . . . Your husband's trips would not be so long nor the exposure so great as where you are [Denver]. . . . Your sickness has given you a gloomy view. . . ."

As well it might. Eventually, her husband's interest in Alaska solved the question of going to Texas, but little else.

One advantage she enjoyed was that he provided his family with financial security. Otherwise, life would have been truly intolerable.

There is no question that she was devoted to him and he to her. Just how much he valued her is indicated by unobtrusive yet frequent evidence scattered throughout his papers. One is a clipping which, while reflecting another missionary's feelings, expressed his own: "I can not tell how many times I have come in from missionary itineracy among the destitute on my field, so sad and weary that I was ready to say, 'I can not go out again from my pleasant home to encounter such toils, privations and hardships,' when her cheerful counsel, her peculiar way of turning 'the bright side' toward me, has re-kindled the missionary spirit, and again toils and privations have been a pleasure. . . . How much do the churches owe to missionary wives. . . ."

What the Church owes to Jackson it owes also to his wife.

CHAPTER 9

STARVATION ON THE YUKON

In August 1896, George Washington Carmack stumbled across rich gold deposits along Bonanza Creek in the Klondike area of Canada. His find produced a chain reaction that resulted in the "rediscovery" of Alaska and sent Sheldon Jackson part-way around the world to organize an expedition to relieve prospectors who had become stranded along the upper waters of the Yukon. The Klondike was a poorly defined region in Canada stretching from below the Klondike River to north of the Indian River just east of the international boundary. The rich, gold-bearing gravel lay in an area eight hundred miles square between the two rivers. Most of the really big claims were located along the streams that flowed into the Klondike and Indian Rivers.

The real significance of Carmack's discovery did not reach the outside world until the summer of 1897 when Jackson was back in Alaska. The Secretary of Agriculture had commissioned him to travel to the upper valley of the Yukon River to survey the agricultural possibilities. He also wanted to see whether moss grew there in sufficient quantities to support reindeer in the event that they should be used to establish routes into the interior. Kjelmann, of the Teller reindeer station, went with him on the Yukon River inspection.

The two men went to St. Michael on Norton Sound to

board the flat-bottomed steamer *Portus B. Weare* for the trip up the Yukon River. When the *Weare* came downriver to St. Michael, it was carrying a half-million-dollar gold cargo, and when the gold reached Oregon aboard the steamer *Portland*, the news of the Klondike strike spread across the nation and the big rush was on to the gold fields.

When the *Weare* started back up the Yukon a few days later, Jackson and Kjelmann were on board. It took twenty days to cover the sixteen hundred miles from the mouth of the river to the headwaters. At some places the river banks were so far apart that neither shore could be seen from the deck of the ship; at other points the river narrowed until it seemed as if one could touch either bank, then spread out again into wide, shallow channels. When Jackson reached Dawson on the Canadian side of the boundary late in July, he found himself in the midst of the turmoil that followed Carmack's original discovery. He remained there a day, then started down river with his notes and specimens of Yukon valley plant life, unaware that the flow of prospectors into the Dawson area would swell to tremendous proportions.

When Jackson returned to St. Michael in August, there was a United States Army officer, Captain P. H. Ray of the Eighth Infantry, waiting in the settlement for upriver transportation to Circle City. Jackson and Ray were not acquainted and neither knew of the other's presence in St. Michael, but the two men were to play major roles in the drama of suffering that was beginning to develop out of the Klondike gold rush. Ray was under orders from the Secretary of War to make a careful and accurate check of reports that miners were starving along the Yukon. Many who headed for the Klondike were unprepared physically, mentally, and emotionally to cope with the climate and the kind of life they had to lead. Many had entered Alaska without sufficient provisions and had become frightened by the lack of supplies in the interior. The letters they wrote to friends and relatives back home were filled with fears that magnified the situation far beyond its actual proportions. In their panic Congress was moved to act at once to relieve the miners. The Chamber of Commerce of Portland, Oregon, informed Washington that the situation in Alaska and the Klondike was desperate, but it had not tried to deter hundreds of Oregonians from setting out for the gold fields. A Citizen's Committee of Tacoma, Washington, organized for the purpose of getting federal assistance, demanded immediate action on behalf of Washingtonians seeking their fortunes in the Klondike. The War Department informed the Senate that information from other sources indicated the existence of a "very serious" food shortage in and around Dawson and asked for authority to get sufficient supplies and clothing into the Klondike to avoid "extreme privation and probably [the] starvation of a great many people. . . ."

But there were those who did not believe that the situation was as bad as it was being depicted. Hugh Wallace, president of the recently organized Chilcoot Railroad and Transportation Company in southeast Alaska, telegraphed the War Department that the reports from Dawson were exaggerated. His company was in the process of constructing a railroad up Dyea Canyon to connect with an aerial tramway over Chilcoot Pass. The line was scheduled for completion by the middle of January 1898. Wallace argued that there would still be plenty of time in January to freight supplies from the tramway terminus to Dawson either by dog sled or reindeer team and that there was no need for any emergency relief. No one in Washington, however, wanted to take responsibility for postponing action because of the clamor being raised across the nation. The Senate took note of the reports of conditions in the Klondike in a resolution passed early in December 1897. Both Houses of

Congresses voted later in the same month to authorize the Secretary of War to purchase supplies and materials to relieve the miners, leaving the Secretary to decide how the provisions should be transported.

The first prospectors to reach the Klondike from the Alaska side came from the Circle City area and the headwaters of Fortymile River in the fall of 1896. When news of the strike reached Juneau and Douglas, other miners went north in the fall and in the spring of 1897. The men who were at St. Michael when the *Weare* came downriver with its gold cargo in 1897 headed up the Yukon for the Klondike. Ray reported from the interior of Alaska in October 1897 that "from what I have learned from mine owners and prospectors, I am fully satisfied that the greater part of the gold lies in our territory, along the ranges known as the Upper Ramparts; that along the Tanana, Manook Creek, Birch Creek, and the head of Forty Mile there are diggings that will pay from ten dollars to twenty dollars per day per man now lying idle. . . . I am satisfied that with adequate means of transportation and cheaper food this will develop into one of the greatest gold producing regions in the world." The Manook Creek "discovery" is dated 1898 while that on the Tanana came in 1902.

Men from the States, who comprised the greater number, entered the Klondike through southeast Alaska. Many went through Skagway at the head of Lynn Canal, climbing dangerous White Pass, crossing the long stretch of frozen lake country beyond the pass which became a swamp in spring and summer, and then proceeding by boat and many portages to Dawson City. Others took the equally difficult route through Dyea, five miles from Skagway, over treacherous Chilcoot Pass, across a wide expanse of glacial ice to Lake Lindeman, and on to Whitehorse. The trail over White Pass was a little shorter, but there was little to choose between the hazards of the one route and those of the other.

From the distance, snow-covered Chilcoot waited, beautifully garbed in a virgin whiteness that hid its treacherous slopes. Those attempting this route stretched in an endless line from Sheep Camp over fifteen miles to Dyea, across a gorge-lined river to the foot of Chilcoot slope, and up over the pass. From below, one could see the dark ascending line of prospectors, at some points scaling the vertical face of the mountain, their feet toed into the hundreds of steps cut into ice and snow by those who had gone before. They would stop and look up at the blinding path they had to climb, measure the grim steps, stare out over the wilderness of mountains and ice extending in all directions, glance below into the glare of the zigzag trail over which they had already traveled, then thrust their shoulders into packs weighing one to two hundred pounds and move painfully up toward the pass.

Jackson had completed his annual inspection of Alaskan missions and schools and was back in Washington by the time Congress directed the War Department to take action. The Secretary of War asked that the agent for education be relieved of his normal duties and assigned to the War Department for the purpose of carrying out the mission ordered by Congress. The Secretary had decided that the only way to get relief to the Yukon area was to organize a reindeer expedition. Since there were not enough animals in Alaska broken to harness for an expedition of the size required, Jackson was instructed to go to Lapland and buy five hundred trained reindeer, sleds, and other necessary equipment, hire the services of fifty drivers, and arrange for the transportation of the animals, sleds, and men to the United States.

It was then four months since Captain Ray had reached

St. Michael en route to the area where starvation conditions had been reported. He found the situation to be somewhat as reported in Washington. Of the eight hundred and forty-eight men who had landed at St. Michael, several hundred were stranded along the Yukon River. About forty had reached the gold fields; others had returned to the States. Although he himself went on to Circle City, Ray stationed his aide, Lieutenant W. P. Richardson, at Fort Yukon to protect the food stored there in warehouses belonging to the river companies. Ray reported to Washington that the companies had not shipped sufficient food to the interior. Less than two thousand tons had been delivered to points above Fort Yukon. Five hundred tons of provisions and liquor had been left at the Fort when low water prevented the steamers from moving upriver.

Shortly after Ray arrived in Circle City, he found a group of miners unloading the cargo from one of the steamers moored there. When he asked the leader of the group how he expected to get away with taking supplies by force, the man pointed to a miner on the deck with a rifle cradled in his arm. It took a lot of persuasion to convince them that they were committing robbery; they believed that they were taking what they needed and would pay for it when they got money. The men argued that they were hungry and that the transportation companies had refused to sell them provisions on credit. When Ray pointed out that there was food at Circle City, they laughed and told him that only thirty tons had been landed by the boat which brought him to Circle City.

Ray took the miners' complaints to the transportation agents with the warning that there would be violence if the companies did not sell food to the miners on credit. In a report to the War Department, he described the background to the food shortage:

"At the present time, neither of the transportation companies will transport a pound of freight for other traders or private parties, forcing all people coming into the Territory to be wholly dependent upon their stores for supplies at their prices. A large majority of the people here now are peaceable and law-abiding, but in the absence of any person in authority to appeal to for the settlement of the many differences that are constantly arising, they are compelled to act outside the law, and when influenced by passion, prejudice, or liquor will commit acts that jeopardize great financial interests and from which there can be no appeal.

"While I consider the situation critical, I do not believe there will be any great loss of life beyond that incident to a climate as rigorous as this. That there will be suffering along the river and the trail owing to the rashness and ignorance of the people, no well-informed person will deny, but there is nothing that should cause undue anxiety or alarm."

The pressure for relief became so great in Circle City that Ray's concern over the possibility of outbreaks mounted each day. About two hundred miners decided that they would go downriver to Fort Yukon to get the provisions and asked the master of one of the steamers at Circle City to make the trip. He told them that the ship was frozen against the landing. When they offered to chop away the ice, he promised to leave as soon as the vessel was free.

One hundred men worked through the night and freed the vessel. But for some reason known only to himself, the master refused to sail. The miners, therefore, decided to seize the ship and make for Fort Yukon themselves. The company agents, when they discovered the plan, went to Ray for help. As soon as he saw the angry crowd at the landing, he knew that his worst fears were about to materialize if something were not done quickly. He told the agents that the only way to avert trouble was to provide the miners with small boats and enough provisions to make the trip. He then called the miners to a meeting. Although he had no means of enforcing his authority, he warned that he would not tolerate any attempt to seize the steamer and that transportation and supplies would be given any man who wanted to leave. After a long and turbulent session, he was able to reassure them that his proposal was best, and by afternoon sixty men had started on the fifteen-hour trip downriver. Ray made arrangements for others to leave as rapidly as possible.

With a sense of apprehension he watched the first boats leave, for he knew that he had averted serious trouble at one place only to court it at another. Several miners had come to him before leaving Circle City with the blunt warning that they did not trust the transportation companies. They made it clear that if conditions at Fort Yukon were not what they were reported to be, they would take matters into their own hands. They would make no further compromises. Ray feared new trouble in the face of these threats because although the company agents claimed there were about one thousand tons of supplies downriver, he knew the amount was closer to three hundred tons.

Ray had mixed emotions about the miners' situation as a result of his observations. He was sharply critical of the fact that the commercial boats used on the Yukon River were not properly designed to do what was required of them. He had worked on the Upper Missouri and Colorado Rivers where low water conditions were frequent, and he told Washington that the Yukon required smaller draft vessels to navigate the shallow sections of river and equipment to get through the flats, particularly during the dry season. He also had doubts about the quality of the crews on these boats, for even if the vessels were capable of river travel, efficient men were needed to handle them.

There was another reason to fear trouble at Fort Yukon. The Canadian Northwest Mounted Police had moved into the Dawson City area when prospectors started flocking to the Klondike in large numbers, both to keep order and to prevent any influx of desperadoes from other areas. The lawless element had left when the Mounted Police arrived and crossed into Alaska where there were no police. None of these unsavory characters came to Circle City, apparently because they knew Ray was there. Instead, they circled around the settlement and headed for Fort Yukon. When Ray discovered where they were going, he knew that Richardson would need his help. Late that afternoon he left Circle City by boat with a small group of men, hoping to reach the Fort by morning.

About eight thirty at night, while the party was having difficulty getting through the thickening river ice, they were startled by a distant roar. An Indian who had joined them said that it was the sound of a great ice mass pushing its way through the river gorge a mile upstream. Soon huge slabs of ice were blocking every effort Ray made to get his boat to shore. They bounced and scraped against the boat, threatening to tumble men and provisions into the river. It was useless to try to steer. When the ice broke two oars, the men could only grip the sides of the boat and hope that the wild, careening ride would end safely. They had no knowledge where they were along the river or whether they were nearer to one shore or the other. About midnight, the boat was hurled out of the water onto an ice jam where it remained upright for a second and then rolled over, spilling men and packs.

Although they had no way of knowing their location, the men were thankful that they were no longer at the mercy of the ice and the river. They spent the remainder of the night crouched in the lee of the boat, shivering in the damp, sharp wind, listening to the passing of the ice. They discovered at dawn that they were stranded on a floe in the middle of the river, with no way of reaching either bank. There was a small island about four hundred yards away; beyond that, it was a quarter of a mile through ice-clogged water to the shore. The other shore was about a half mile away with no possibility of reaching it.

When it got lighter and they were able to get a better look upriver, the party spotted several boats, abandoned along a three-quarter mile stretch of the river. But there were no signs of the miners who had left Circle City. Later in the day they saw a group of men on the right bank and shouted for help; but the roar of the water drowned out their cries, and the men disappeared into the timber, evidently on their way downstream. Disconsolately they stood around the boat, not knowing what to do. Then one of the party walked to the edge of the ice pack on which they were stranded and picked his way slowly and carefully across a narrow stretch of ice in the direction of the island. Ray shouted to him to come back, but the man waved his arm and went on. Halfway to the island he stopped and hurried back, slipping and sliding on the uneven surface to report that the ice might be firm enough for them to reach the island.

Ray questioned the man sharply, but he argued that despite the danger it was better to make the effort than to remain where they were. An unexpected warm spell would break up the ice pack on which they were stranded. Furthermore, the island would be a better vantage point from which to attract the attention of anyone on the shore.

They left all the gear that was not needed, preferring to lose it rather than their food, and started out single file, moving slowly and carefully over the rough surface. It was dangerously thin in spots; at one point they almost stopped and retraced their steps. But moving on turned out to be the wisest decision in the end. When they were all across to the island, Ray went to its highest point and spotted a tiny wisp of smoke on shore. Then he saw what looked like another of the boats that had left Circle City earlier. Several of the men joined him, and together they shouted and waved for a half hour. Just when they were worn out and ready to give up, the men at the camp saw them. Even then, it was by no means certain that they would get help because of the danger of rowing out to the island. Those on shore did attempt the rescue, however, and just before dark the last of Ray's party reached land and crowded around the campfire to get warm. Their rescuers were part of the first group that had left Circle City. They had run their boat into shore when they became afraid of the ice in the river. They told Ray that some of the miners had started downstream on the opposite shore; many others were stranded up and down the river below the campsite, which was sixty-five miles above Fort Yukon and about twenty-five miles below Circle City. A check of the shore line the following day disclosed about one hundred and fifty miners, most of them without food or clothing. Only two were rescued from midstream before a warm spell broke up the ice and ended the possibility of further rescue work. All through the night there were cries for help from out on the river, but Ray and his men could do nothing but sit helplessly by, never knowing when some of those who were calling for help had drowned.

Ray sent an Indian and a white prospector down the river to Richardson with an urgent plea for relief supplies as quickly as possible. The white man came back to camp late at night in a state of exhaustion. The ice in the river had raised the water in the sloughs, forcing him and his companion to make long detours through the knee-deep snow in the forest. When the miner realized that he would never reach Fort Yukon, he turned back while he still had enough strength to reach the camp. The Indian got to Richardson with Ray's message, but it took him three and a half days and he was half dead from exposure and lack of food. Richardson dispatched two dog teams loaded with supplies early the next morning in charge of two white men and another Indian. The white men reached Ray's camp five days later with only a part of the supplies, explaining to the captain that they had given half to hungry miners they met on the trail and left most of the remainder with the Indian to distribute to other stragglers on their way to Fort Yukon. It seemed doubtful that all of the miners would reach the settlement, but they did, many of them more dead than alive. One group appeared on the other side of the river from the Fort and were ferried across. Most of their gear had been abandoned at the outset because they were too weak to carry it. The little food they had been able to keep had been eaten the first two days of the trip. For the next two, they had lived on a mixture of cold water and flour. They had been without food the last two days.

A second group arrived at Fort Yukon that night, and several more prospectors reached the settlement during the following days. Some of them were in better physical shape than others, particularly the more experienced; but all had one thought in common: to destroy anything that belonged to the transportation companies. Their feeling was compounded of fear, anger, and defeat, for they believed that they had been left to the mercy of the country by those who should have helped them. Not one was willing to admit that he had any responsibility for his own condition or that he might have been totally unprepared for what he had to face.

Richardson's experience was the same as Ray's. It was impossible to reason with any of the prospectors. Most of them were without clothing, food, or the means of earning money to buy what they needed. Since there was not enough at Fort

Yukon, the rapidly approaching winter spelled new disaster. Richardson talked the company agents into issuing emergency rations and lending tents and stoves to provide temporary shelter for the miners.

Would-be prospectors who had been forced to stay at Fort Yukon because they had not been able to get transportation to Dawson City added their dissatisfaction to the ugly mood of those returning. Groups gathered every day to discuss their plight and give vent to their ire; there was open talk of attacking the warehouses so that the men could take what they wanted. Richardson's difficulty was that there was no one else in authority to whom he could turn for help. He doubted that anyone could have enforced law and order even if he had had the badge of his office. The only recourse, as he saw it, was to prod the company into making some kind of compromise with the prospectors. He succeeded in getting them to issue rations on a credit basis with the argument that most of the miners, however disgruntled, were reasonable and would respond to fair treatment. Worst of all, the able-bodied were without work. Richardson met that problem by working out an agreement whereby the companies provided a month's provisions and clothing to those who would go into the forest and cut cord wood on a contract basis. This maneuver succeeded in getting those out of the settlement who might have taken supplies by violence.

Meanwhile, Ray's situation was no better than when he had sent to Richardson for help. There were still about one hundred men scattered above and below the camp, all in desperate need. Several who had come better prepared contributed their supplies to a common larder and agreed to go out and bring stragglers to the camp. But the captain found himself facing an almost unresolvable problem. He had no way of knowing how many men were at Fort Yukon or how many supplies

Richardson could spare. His own meager stores were sufficient for no more than eight days if they were doled out carefully. Reports he had received of trail conditions from the first relief party convinced him that it would take at least a week for any of the men in his vicinity to reach the Fort. Each day brought the threat of new snow and a worsening of the dilemma. He finally decided to send a second message to Richardson asking him to dispatch another relief group while he started the miners downriver to meet the rescue party. There were about a hundred men stumbling through the forest by nightfall of October 14. As a result of Richardson's quick response to Ray's request, everyone made the trip safely. All were hungry, many were sick, but the strategy had paid off.

The day he reached Fort Yukon, Captain Ray made arrangements for feeding and housing the sick and indigent at government expense. An inventory of supplies on hand at settlement confirmed his doubts: it would take the most careful handling to make the provisions on hand last until more could be shipped in. Two days later, he received a warning that a gang who had fled from the Canadian authorities were collecting rifles and ammunition to attack the warehouses. Ray had no way to meet the emergency but by bluff. He served notice that he was taking over all stores in the name of the federal government and would shoot anyone who tried to pilfer the warehouses. Then he posted an armed guard where he could be seen by everyone but warned the man not to risk his life in trying to repel an attack.

Ray and Richardson spent an uneasy afternoon and night while they waited for the sound of rifle fire. By dawn they knew that the deception had worked and that the men from whom they had the most to fear had headed farther west.

By the end of October Ray reported to Washington that

he had several hundred men on his hands who would be thoroughly dependent upon the supplies at Fort Yukon for the next seven months. About half were at the settlement or in the immediate vicinity; the remainder were scattered at campsites along the river. By rationing food at three pounds a day, without tea or coffee, Ray thought there would be enough to feed nine hundred men until June 1. Under normal conditions this would have been enough, but it was hardly sufficient to sustain men in the interior of Alaska, particularly those who were doing any kind of work. Ray eventually had to take over the provisions and stores of both transportation companies in the name of the Government to avoid trouble and to maintain an effective rationing system.

His reports to his superiors are examples of amazing restraint, particularly important for what they have to say about conditions in general in the territory. They are an objective evaluation of the problems with which Jackson and others had to contend in their efforts to develop Alaska. Ray not only reported what he saw but documented his observations with interviews with those whom he called "permanent" settlers and miners. He concluded that people feared the inadequacy and, in some areas, complete lack of transportation facilities more than they feared starvation. This was one result of Washington's refusal to survey the territory and to provide the financial support needed by private groups for developing rail and road facilities. The chaotic state of the territorial government, the lack of good civil and criminal codes, laxity in opening the way to homesteading, the general uncertainties of life which impeded the development of new industries—all worked together to deter American capital from investing in transportation. Every Alaskan was aware of the fact that Canadian authorities were cognizant of the territory's business potential and were willing to help British business interests in the organization of two-way rail traffic between the Alaskan interior and the outside world.

Ray reported from Circle City that "the people here are now afraid that the failure of the Yukon River route for freight will cause the construction of a railroad through British North America to the Yukon River above the boundary, and that the mining districts of Alaska will be dependent for supplies on a route through a foreign country with all that means in the way of discrimination in favor of British merchants."

When Congress passed a law in May 1898 which contained general provisions for railroad construction in Alaska, the British-owned White Pass and Yukon Railroad filed a right of way in Alaska. It eventually connected Skagway in southeast Alaska with Whitehorse in the Canadian Yukon, twenty miles of the line running through American territory and the remaining ninety-two in Canada. When Congress levied taxes on Alaskan business in 1899, the rate on railroads was one hundred dollars for every operating mile, "thus perpetuating the monopoly of the White Pass which was the only one that could afford to pay that amount," according to Nichols. Exactly how much of a monopoly may be a moot question. There was a wagon route from Haines to the Yukon which carried freight and there were river boats on the Yukon connecting the interior of Alaska with St. Michael, though they could not operate all year. Nichols says that after the completion of the White Pass in 1900 it was the only railroad for two decades that led to the interior of Alaska; Gruening makes it twenty-four years. The Copper River and Northwestern Railroad was completed in 1910, running from Cordova to Chitina to Kennecott, a distance of 196 miles, and several other short lines were either projected or under construction in the early 1900's. Apparently, Nichols and Gruening were thinking in terms of a much longer American route to the interior, such as the government-owned Alaska Railroad, completed in June 1923, which ran 540 miles from Seward to Fairbanks.

Ray coupled his plea in October 1897 for "adequate means of transportation and cheaper food" by proposing that the government make a preliminary survey of a railroad route "from the head of Cook's Inlet or Prince William Sound to the mouth of the Tanannah [*sic*], from which point supplies could be delivered by light-draft steamers along all the navigable tributaries of the Yukon." This route, he believed, would "secure to our own people the commerce of this whole country. It would give a route to the open sea that could be operated all winter, and act as a check to the Canadian route." The Alaska Railroad followed approximately the route Ray proposed, except that it terminated at Fairbanks, farther to the east of the juncture of the Tanana and Yukon Rivers.

Ray also proposed the establishment of a military government in Alaska as a means of combating the lack of law enforcement until such time as an effective civil government could impose its authority, particularly in the remote areas of the territory. He placed the blame for many of Alaska's social and economic perplexities upon the absence of any clear-cut demonstration of United States authority, and he had absorbed enough of the pessimism of Alaskans to believe that it would be a long time before respect for the law could be achieved otherwise. Under such circumstances a military "big stick" would be preferable to government-by-vacuum. He was more than a little chagrined over the fact that while he had been trying to protect the food stocks at Fort Yukon, a transportation company warehouse there had been robbed of more than six thousand dollars in gold dust. The theft caused hardly a ripple, largely because of the total apathy toward authority.

The condition of the mail system was symptomatic of the general state of affairs in the territory. The regular mail contractor for the interior made delivery to Circle City only once during 1897. Not one sack of mail left the settlement in either direction throughout the same year nor were there plans for sending mail west to Circle City during the winter. Ray reported that he had no knowledge of the whereabouts of the Circle City postmaster except that he was somewhere in the States, his assistant having been removed from office because of drunkenness. It was almost beside the point that the Post Office Department had not provided stamps for the interior since mail sent east from St. Michael was on its own, with no one designated to see to its delivery. There were no route agents, and the transportation companies paid little or no attention to it.

Shortly after his return to Fort Yukon, he discovered that one hundred bags of mail had been dropped on the landing and left there. He induced the master of the *Weare* to take some, but the captain of the *Bella* refused to touch a single letter. Some time later, Ray was walking near the river's edge when he stumbled over a sack, half-buried by the snow, that contained several hundred letters addressed to persons in the Dawson area. He had no way of knowing how long it had been there. That was in October. When he included an account of this finding in his report, he added that he hoped to get the sack forwarded to its destination by the spring of the following year.

Ray suggested drastic measures to prevent a repetition of the Klondike troubles. He urged the federal government in November 1897 to ban anyone from entering the interior who could not support himself for at least two years because there would be no means of earning money to buy provisions. He underscored his remedy by pointing out that there had not been a single discovery of a new placer district of any importance on either side of the boundary during the last six months of 1897. All Klondike claims of any value had been filed. Ray believed that fewer than seven per cent of all the men who had entered the interior in 1897 were earning their own living by the year's end. Hundreds were scattered along the Yukon, Klondike, and Indian Rivers and their tributaries —low on food, clothing, money and morale. He saw no likelihood of any change in their situation for at least a year. Approximately twelve hundred men were camped at various places along the Yukon River between the Tanana and the Canadian line. Fifty per cent were without either jobs or the means to work at what was available. A large percentage of those who had come to Fort Yukon for assistance had families in the States who were dependent on them for support while they themselves were stranded. Ray was fearful that even though the food situation was under control, the steady deterioration of the men's spirits, the lack of authority to protect life and property, and the ever-present resentment toward the transportation companies might lead to new disorders. The fact that most wrongdoers could escape punishment added to the temptation of many to take what they believed had been denied to them by a cruel and unjust fate.

The natives of the interior were also in a sorry predicament —not a little of it the direct result of the gold rush. Ray reported that bands of Indians were starving to death. Women and children died on the trail as the tribes tried to reach settlements. Ray himself rescued a group of about one hundred and forty men, women, and children in one area and another eighty elsewhere. All were physically wasted and unable to help themselves. One cause of their plight was that the caribou migration had by-passed the Indians' normal hunting grounds, and a bad fish catch the previous season had added to the food shortage. To a large degree, however, Ray blamed the "gold craze" for their impoverished state. The trader at Fort Yukon who took care of most of the Indians in the region reported that he had been unable to have sufficient stores delivered during the summer of 1897 because "the mining interest assumed such magnitude as practically to obliterate the Indian trading interests, and no attention was paid to supplying the natives with arms, ammunition, blankets." Even where the companies did have supplies, Ray reported that prices were so high the Indians could not pay them.

In his report to Washington of January 13, 1898, he wrote that "up-to-date there is nothing in sight or reported to justify the great excitement the discoveries in Northwest Territory started, or to avert a collapse of the many schemes now being promoted in the States to float stock based on alleged mines in Alaska. The advertising given this country by the newspapers, the transportation companies, and mining companies has become criminal in view of the distress and suffering it has caused."

Ray left the interior by way of Dawson on February 13, 1898. On his way to Washington State he saw enough to convince him that there was no starvation along the Yukon or at Dawson nor any destitution that had not been relieved, but he judged there were about eight to ten thousand persons still on their way into the Klondike region by way of Skagway and Chilcoot Pass. In May 1898, Captain Ray reported that "the whole country in the Klondike district has been staked out and there has not been any new rich discovery made in the Northwest Territory since the Klondike strike, so that many good paying districts in Alaska that were abandoned when the Klondike rush occurred are now being relocated.

The most noted are Birch Creek, Seventy Mile, American Creek, and Mission Creek. . . . It is well known that there are extensive districts along the Tanana, Koyukuk, Porcupine, Juan de Leur (Chandelar) that will pay from twelve dollars to twenty dollars per day per man, but none are being worked as such claims can not be made to pay with the present price of food. . . ."

The conclusion to be drawn from Ray's reports is that the claims of imminent starvation among the miners were exaggerated, and that was the conclusion reached by those who read the reports at the time they were made. But his first dispatches left some uncertainty about the exact state of affairs. Since, too, there was considerable lapse of time beween the writing of the reports and their delivery in Washington, it is understandable that the Secretary of War should have proceeded with the plan to send Jackson to Lapland. Ray's final reports were on hand before Jackson returned, making it clear that there was no need for proceeding with the relief expedition. This was an unfortunate turn of events because the United States Commissioner of Education had asked Congress in 1897 to appropriate forty-five thousand dollars to buy additional animals and establish new reindeer stations in Alaska, a request which had provoked a new storm of newspaper criticism.

An incident which also took place in 1897 turned out to be one of the best answers ever given to critics of the reindeer program. Jackson had just returned to Washington from his annual inspection trip to Alaska when reports reached the capital that three hundred sailors were stranded in the Arctic after a fleet of whaling vessels had been crushed in the ice. The government refuge station at Point Barrow was all that stood between the survivors and death. But no one had ever thought that so many men would descend on the station at one time, so there was neither enough food nor adequate facilities. Sanitary conditions became so bad that disease threatened to wipe out all three hundred even before starvation had its effect. The disaster caused such a furor that President McKinley called a cabinet meeting to discuss relief measures and invited Jackson to participate. Jackson pointed out that there was no hope of getting a rescue ship even as far as Cape Prince of Wales. He did believe that a revenue steamer could get as far north as Point Rodney, close enough to Cape Prince of Wales so that a rescue team could be put ashore for an overland trek to the reindeer station at the Cape. From that point Lopp, the manager of the station, could drive his herd to Barrow to provide fresh meat for the men marooned there.

Jackson suggested that three officers of the *Bear*, including the ship's surgeon, make the trip to Barrow. He had complete confidence in their knowledge of the Arctic region and in their personal courage. Nor was there any question in his mind about Lopp's ability to handle his part of the assignment, President McKinley, having no alternative to Jackson's plan, ordered it put into effect. The *Bear* cleared Port Townsend and, as was to be expected, ran into blinding snow. One storm after another pounded her as she steamed through the North Pacific into the Gulf of Alaska until it became evident that the vessel would never reach Point Rodney. She therefore waited off Cape Vancouver for the weather to clear sufficiently so that the three officers could land and start the eight-hundred-mile trip overland to the reindeer station, stopping at mission stations enroute for supplies and rest.

For one thousand miles from Cape Prince of Wales to Barrow, Lopp drove his herd of four hundred and thirty-five reindeer with the assistance of several native herdsmen. The route skirted Good Hope Bay at the southeastern end of

Kotzebue Bay, through a pass in the Waring Mountains, over the Baird Range, across the frozen tundra east of Point Hope, and up the coastal region past Icy Cape, Cape Collie, and Franklin Point. The expedition reached its objective on March 29, and not a day too soon.

More than half of the men were seriously ill. But within a week the sickest began to show improvement, and with the change in their diet and the correction of the sanitation trouble, the crisis came to an end. The *Bear* was not able to reach Barrow until the following summer, but the difference in morale that followed the arrival of the relief party made it possible for all of the men to survive. As a secondary result of the mission, a herd was established at Point Barrow to forestall any future large-scale emergency. This also helped to convert the Eskimo economy above the Arctic Circle as had already been done farther south.

President McKinley's statement on the success of the venture was full of praise for the three officers, but he failed to say anything about the contribution made by Lopp and his group. An even more glaring omission was his failure to recognize the part played by Jackson. It had been his foresight in the first place which had made the plan workable.

The year 1897 did, however, bring honor to Jackson. He was elected to the highest office the Presbyterian church could give him—that of moderator of the General Assembly. The speech that placed his name in nomination was probably one of the shortest of its kind. One of the seconding addresses supplied the rhetoric and the tributes to his achievements; another proclaimed him "the greatest missionary the world [has] ever seen since the Apostle Paul went far hence unto the Gentiles and died upon the scaffold. . . ." His opponents were men of considerable stature, including former President Benjamin Harrison and John Wanamaker, but the unclericallooking Jackson won on the first ballot. That was in May 1897, just after his birthday. Two weeks after his election, he was back at his desk in Washington. In another month he was on his way up the Yukon River Valley. Before the end of 1897 he was on his way to Lapland.

CHAPTER 10

LAPLAND TO ALASKA

Jackson left Washington for Lapland two days before Christmas 1897. As he waited in front of his office building for a cab to take him to the railroad station, the cold, damp wind chilled every bone in his body and made him wish that he was at home instead of starting on a journey that was certain to produce many hardships. At almost any other time in his life he would have plunged with relish into the assignment he had received, but of late he had felt more tired than usual. He pulled the muffler more tightly about his throat, picked up his bags, and walked toward the approaching cab with the steps of a man whose energies were beginning to wane. No sooner was he seated when a sharp pain flashed into his side. When it had subsided, he leaned back and wiped the sweat from his forehead. It was not the first attack that he had suffered; he hoped that, whatever it was that bothered him, it would not recur soon. Anyone seeing him walk briskly through the railroad station would not have guessed at the will power it took to keep him going. Twice he had to ask the ticket seller for the price of the fare to New York. The clerk leaned forward and almost spelled it out for him—three dollars and twenty-five cents for the first class seat and two dollars extra for the sleeping car berth.

The next morning he had an early breakfast on the train

while he made notes of the things he had to do before boarding the Cunard liner *Lucania* that night. When he had reached New York and sent his baggage to the pier, he went to two steamship companies to see if he could charter a ship for the return trip. But neither was able to satisfy him, and he left the question of return passage to be decided when he reached London. His next stop was the freight department of the Pennsylvania Railroad to see about hauling the reindeer west after they were landed in New York. Late in the morning he headed uptown for a meeting at the offices of the Board of Home Missions. This was followed by another conference concerned with the future of the work at Point Barrow and by a meeting with the officers of the Women's Board of Home Missions. Late in the afternoon he had to attend to some personal matters. After a solitary supper he returned to the board rooms to discuss more business. That night, on board the ship, he was visited by Army Lieutenant D. B. Devoe, who had been assigned to help him handle the details involved in bringing the shipment back to the States. They talked for a while, then parted after arranging to meet at breakfast to go over a few other details.

Jackson was up at five thirty the next morning, Christmas Day, so that he could get a morning newspaper. When the ship backed away from the pier at six thirty, it was coated with ice as a result of the storm that had struck during the night. Jackson and Devoe went out on the promenade deck after breakfast. It was a bright day, clear and cold. The sea was smooth, but they had to forego a walk because the deck was too slippery. The next day at dinner Jackson gave Devoe a briefing on what he had learned from reading Stoddard's *Lectures on Norway* and described his excellent experience with the Laplanders who worked at the reindeer stations in Alaska from 1893 to 1895. Devoe was relieved when he discovered that Kjelmann, the Teller Station superintendent, had been sent to Norway for the purpose of hiring a new group of Lapp instructors for Alaska before Jackson received his Lapland assignment. It had taken only a cable to instruct him to expand his mission and start the roundup of animals and sleds.

Fame always had a way of catching up with Jackson despite his efforts to avoid it. Just as he was congratulating himself that no one on board the *Lucania* knew his identity, someone discovered who he was. In no time he found himself with an invitation to give a lecture on board ship about Alaska, the Yukon River Valley, and the Klondike. He accepted even though he had hoped for a quiet trip, free from what he described as the unceasing drive of the last few months.

The weather took a turn for the worst when the ship was two days out of New York and remained bad throughout the rest of the trip, one storm following another. By the time they reached the Irish Channel, the fog was inky black. The ship hardly dared to move while it sounded an incessant, mournful warning of its presence. Those who were on deck at the time stared in shock when their steamer passed close by the masts of a vessel that had gone down in the previous day's storm.

The *Lucania* docked on the afternoon of December 31. Immediately after Jackson and Devoe had passed through customs, they met shipping agents who had come to the pier to discuss arrangements for the trip back to New York. They all adjourned to the company's offices to continue the talks, but when no agreement could be reached, Jackson and Devoe caught the evening train for London. They went directly to the Cecil Hotel where they had accommodations—or at least they thought they had. The management assigned them to three different suites before the mix-up was settled.

The New Year started with a problem that was merely a warning of other difficulties to come. Jackson and Devoe went to the British Ministry of Agriculture to see what procedures had to be followed in transshipping the reindeer; they learned that a quarantine had been imposed on all animals from Scandinavia as the result of hoof and mouth disease among cattle in southern Sweden. Jackson asked if he could keep the animals on board ship while the vessel was in an English port, but that too was impossible because the government had quarantined even the ships that carried stock from Scandinavia to England. Therefore he had to change his plans and charter a boat that would take the reindeer directly from Lapland to the United States. Although it meant a delay and a complete revision of schedule, he had no alternative. As a result, Devoe had to remain in England to arrange for transportation while Jackson went on to Lapland alone.

On the Sunday morning before his departure for Scandinavia, Jackson went with Devoe to hear the preaching of the Rev. Monro Gibson of St. John's Wold Presbyterian Church. Dr. Gibson introduced Jackson as the moderator of the Presbyterian Church in the United States and then invited him and the lieutenant to dinner. After dinner they attended afternoon services at Westminster Abbey. That night they went to City Temple to hear the Rev. Joseph Parker preach, but they arrived a little late, the only places to sit were on the gallery stairs. They had been there for a few moments when Jackson noticed that a nearby pew was not quite as full as the others. He thought about it for a moment and then beckoned to an usher. Handing the man his calling card, he pointed to the words "Moderator, Presbyterian Church, U.S.A.," and asked if he would try to make room for him in the pew. The usher in turn passed the card to the people in the pew. After they had all looked at it, they moved over and made room for Jackson. But Devoe sat through the service on the gallery stairs.

Jackson reached Copenhagen on January 5 where he boarded a train for Christiania. It was a rainy, disagreeable day. When they reached Göteborg, the conductor brought him a pair of woolen blankets and a small pillow so that he could make a bed for himself on the seven-foot seat. He went to sleep as the first snow was settling over the countryside.

The American consul in Christiania introduced him to Norwegian officials who provided letters of instruction to local officers in Lapland, directing them to give him all the assistance he needed. He traveled by train to Trondheim and boarded a steamer for the remainder of the journey. As he watched the coast slip by and became aware of the hazards of sea travel in that part of the world, he inwardly compared the navigation aids existing along the Norwegian shore line to the lack of such aids along the Alaskan coast, for as the vessel passed out of sight of one lighthouse, it picked up another in the distance. There were no such guides for shipping in Alaska. He noted too the extent of communication in Norway. Every important village up to North Cape had mail service and either telegraph or telephone contact with the rest of the world; there was even a telegraph line that extended above the Arctic Circle. By contrast, he reflected, much of Alaska was isolated not only from the outside world but also from itself.

When the steamer put in at Tromsoe, Jackson took the opportunity to see a town under lights at midday, for it was the time of year (between November 18 and the end of January) when the days are one with the nights. He was surprised to find that a businessman on whom he called had gone home at two in the afternoon for dinner and a nap and would not return to his office until four. It was a practice followed by all business and government offices. Jackson was thrilled by his visit to Tromsoe, then the northernmost point in Norway to have electricity. His only disappointment was that school was not in session, for he hoped to learn something about Norwegian methods and curriculum.

He was rowed ashore at Alten, or Bosekop, and driven by sleigh to his hotel. Having greeted the owner, he was chagrined to find that the man did not understand English. There they were, standing in the foyer making efforts to understand each other. It was the innkeeper who gave up the struggle, picked up Jackson's bags, then put them down and motioned for the missionary to give him his hat and coat. What with the two of them trying to outdo each other in courteousness, it was a few seconds before arms were untangled and the guest was shown to his room. There they went through the same frustrating charade until the host departed, leaving Jackson to acquaint himself with his quarters. It was a bright and cheery place with a good view of the town, but it was also a little colder than he had expected. The bed, large enough for several people his size, was piled high with covers. He pulled back a white spread, which reached almost to the floor, to admire the linen sheet, beautifully embroidered at both ends. Beneath the sheet were two woolen blankets, under them another linen sheet, and under that a soft eiderdown cover for the mattress.

At breakfast the next morning he found that several letters and telegrams had come for him. After going through another sign-language session, he set out for the telegraph office with some vague idea about its location. Fortunately, the telegraph operator did know English.

It occurred to him while he was writing out the telegrams that he might have found the answer to the language barrier. Having finished his business, he talked with the operator long enough to find out that his English was good and then worked out an arrangement that proved to be very effective. Jackson would write in English whatever it was that he wanted to do or buy, and the telegrapher would put the Norwegian translation below. Armed with his bilingual aid, he was able to go from store to store making purchases and to communicate with people like the hotel proprietor. The services of the telegraph operator would have been valuable the afternoon that the local Roman Catholic priest came to call. The two clergymen sat in Jackson's room, struggling to be affable in spite of their inability to say anything that the other understood. After frustrating minutes, the priest spoke a few words in Latin to Jackson, who responded with a smile because he recognized the language. Unfortunately, he could not make head or tail out of what his visitor was trying to say—except for a few words—and in the end the priest gave up the effort and made his departure. As Jackson phrased it, the conversation had not been very free or exciting.

His inability to speak Norwegian became the least of his worries after two days had passed in Alten. Then he began to worry about Kjelmann's whereabouts. The Teller superintendent was two days overdue in meeting him, and when it started to snow heavily, Jackson was fearful that some accident might have befallen his friend in the mountains north of the town. It did not help his peace of mind to learn that it was very difficult to come through the mountain passes once the first snow had fallen. He even started to worry about the Laplanders whom Kjelmann had hired to help round up reindeer and recruit drivers. Day after day Jackson watched the never-ending storm. He could feel the two-story hotel rock on its wide, stone foundations as the wind picked up in intensity. If it was impossible to see more than a few yards in the village, it would be even worse in the mountains.

Kjelmann finally arrived in Alten the next day, covered with snow and ice from the brim of his cap to the soles of his boots. It had taken him two days to get through the mountains after losing the trail. He had ridden two days and nights without rest, but his condition and report were good. Drivers were being recruited. Five hundred animals were grouped in several herds and would be brought through the pass as soon as the weather moderated. Kjelmann took a couple of days to thaw out before returning to the mountains to oversee the transport of the animals into town. He arrived back in Alten with the first herd on the afternoon of January 28 in the midst of a blinding snowstorm that was so bad even Jackson had to stay in the hotel. The weather was also having its effect on the Lapps who had agreed to go to Alaska. The two men discussed this newest development in Jackson's room.

"I don't know whether we can get them to make the trip." Kjelmann nodded toward the blanket that Jackson had hung over the window to keep out the cold. "Look at that curtain." It was billowing into the room. "Can you imagine what it's like up in the mountains? It's way below freezing and the snow is getting very deep."

"But they are accustomed to such weather, aren't they?" Jackson asked.

"Yes, but in their own country. And they stay at home during storms like the one we're having. If they go with us they will have to bring their families across the mountains in weather that even the men don't want to face."

"How many Lapps have agreed to go to Alaska?"

"If none of them back out, and now it's hard to say what's going to happen, there are forty-three Lapps, fifteen Norwegians, and ten Finns."

"How many families and children does that mean?"

Kjelmann took a pad out of his pocket and checked the figures.

"Sixteen of the Lapps are married, so that makes sixteen women. And nineteen children. Most of them are very young, and it is particularly because of them that their parents are balking."

"I don't blame them," Jackson said. "It must be hard enough to leave their homes, but to do it in weather like this!" He felt the cold draft sweeping through the room and re-adjusted one of the blankets.

"Are any of the others married?" he asked.

"Yes. Three of the Norwegians, and they have seven children between them, but none of the Finns are married." Kjelmann flipped over a page to check the list of Lapps. "I'm not certain, but at least two or three of the Lapp drivers have just gotten married."

"That means we'll have some bridal parties with us on the trip, won't we?"

"Yes. But in the long run the newlyweds may be the ones who will back out."

"Are the terms of the contracts that they signed exactly what we agreed they should be?" Jackson asked.

"The same," Kjelmann answered. "At least as nearly as I remember." He took several sheets of folded paper from his pocket. "I have the terms written down so you can check as to whether they are correct." He read slowly, pausing between items to get confirmation from Jackson.

"Each man is to work as reindeer herder, driver, and tanner, and to instruct the Eskimos in all details of raising reindeer. Each man is to get a loan of one hundred reindeer for three to five years with the original number of reindeer to be returned to the government station at the end of the contract period." He stopped and asked Jackson if that were correct.

"Yes, it is. You remember that we worked out a similar arrangement with the first group of Laplanders who came to Alaska so that if they wanted to remain in the territory they would have a herd of their own."

Kjelman resumed, reading the contract arrangement.

". . . salaries to be continued in event of illness . . . free schooling for their children . . . no taxes for the duration of the contracts which must run no less than two years . . . no military service required . . . free light and heat and washing and mending of clothing for the single men . . . those with wives get provisions once a month . . . the single men the same arrangement for supplies but a cook to prepare their meals . . . no Sunday work except what is absolutely needed . . . free transportation to Alaska . . . all necessary and required food and clothing provided except tobacco . . . salary $22.33 a month . . . plus all other things necessary for existence. . . ."

He refolded the papers.

"That's it."

"That's what we agreed," Jackson confirmed. "Now, all we need is the reindeer and the drivers and the herdsmen to get started back."

"What ship do you have?" Kjelmann asked.

"We've chartered the *Manitoban*. She's a 1,865-ton iron steamship with accommodations for two hundred steerage passengers. The master is a captain Andrew Broes. Lieutenant Devoe has written me that he is a very fine person, a veteran of more than forty years sailing the Atlantic. The only thing that I am afraid of is that the ship will be overdue. Today is the thirtieth and it should have been here by now."

"Don't worry about it. The weather is responsible, and by the time the Lapps bring the herds into town and they make up their minds to go with us, the *Manitoban* should be here."

Kjelmann and Jackson spent the next two days in Alten

waiting anxiously for the *Manitoban*'s arrival. Meanwhile two more herds were driven across the mountains into the town, and several Lapp families arrived. On the third morning, Jackson walked out of the hotel and discovered that the ship had entered the harbor during the night. He rushed back to get Kjelmann, and the two men hastened to the dock to get started with the work of building pens on the ship's deck. That same day the last of the animals were brought into town, followed by all of the herders who had signed contracts. During the next two days everyone was busy loading three hundred animals, two hundred sleds, and a large supply of baled moss aboard the vessel. On February 4, when the remaining animals and equipment were on board and Jackson had ordered the herders to board the steamer, Kjelmann brought him bad news. Some of the drivers had been drinking and were refusing to board the *Manitoban* until an inventory was made of their belongings.

Jackson replied that the request was impossible, that the ship had to get under way, and that the inventory could be made later.

"I know that and I told them so, but they won't listen."

Half an hour later, at Jackson's request, the police came to the staging area and told the Lapps that they had their choice of boarding the vessel or going to jail. By the deadline set for ending the impasse, everyone had co-operated. When the mail steamer arrived that evening from Hammerfest, Kjelmann discovered that it carried four kegs of whiskey for delivery to the Lapps. He had the police confiscate it, and it was well that he did because with the few bottles of whiskey the Lapps managed to bring on board the *Manitoban* they produced pandemonium in the steerage for several hours.

Jackson also had serious troubles of his own. Climbing the hill back to the hotel to get his own bags packed, he suffered a severe attack of rheumatism in his knee. For days he had been standing in the cold, damp wind supervising every phase of the loading, and it had been too much for him. By the time he was finished packing, he was unable to stand, let alone walk to the dock. He had to be taken to the pier by sleigh, almost carried into a small boat, and helped aboard the *Manitoban* like a cripple.

To make matters worse, his stateroom was like nothing he had ever seen. The berth was damp with the condensation of the warm air against the cold wall. One end of the bed was so wet that it could not be used. Little puddles of water were everywhere on the floor, the result of water dripping through the ceiling. Fearing that if he once got into the berth he would not be able to get out of it, he hobbled around the room for several hours, trying to put away his clothing. The moment the ship got under way, he felt much better. But he was shortly to realize that he was in for a miserable trip. The second day at sea the ship ran into a storm that left two inches of snow on the decks. The ocean was relatively smooth, but many of the Lapps were horribly seasick and lay on the open deck despite every effort to get them down to the steerage. Jackson's own physical condition gradually improved enough so that by Sunday, February 6, he was prepared to hold services for anyone who cared to attend. It was a useless effort. A heavy southeast swell rolled the vessel endlessly from one side to the other, making the herdsmen sicker than before and bringing Jackson so close to being ill himself that he had to spend the day pacing up and down the deck despite the lurching of the steamer.

The *Manitoban* passed between the Faroe Islands and Iceland the following day. With the continuing bad weather, many of the sick Lapps stayed on the open deck throughout the night. The sixth day of the trip heavy seas began to cascade over the hurricane deck aft of the bridge. The pens which had been built there to hold the animals were extremely stout. But when furious waves began to smash the two-inch planking, the deer had to be removed from the damaged area and taken aft. Meanwhile, the *Manitoban* plunged and pounded through the rough seas. By February 11 wind and sea were battering the steamer so severely that Jackson feared every seam would open. Snow and hail storms slammed across the decks; under the hammerlike blows of the sea the ship shuddered violently. The water continued to sweep over the bow, swirling knee-deep the length of the deck and endangering more of the animals, who had to be removed to safer quarters. Captain Broes admitted that he had never been through such a succession of violent storms in all the years he had sailed the North Atlantic. Water which had leaked through the ceiling from the pens overhead was awash in Jackson's cabin up to the ankles. Nothing was dry.

Despite his own discomfiture he felt particularly upset about conditions among the drivers and their families in the steerage. He had gone down there during one lull in the weather and found it wet, greasy, and filthy. Later three cases of measles developed, and all the Lapps, Norwegians, and Finns had to be examined to see if they had been innoculated. Only a few of the younger children had not. Two more cases were found the next day. By then, however, the worst of the trip was over. The ship's doctor was able to cure the sick and prevent the spread of the disease. The vessel was off Sandy Hook on February 28, a little more than two months after Jackson had passed the same point on his way to Europe.

The expedition was entrained in New York for Seattle, where reindeer, herdsmen, and equipment were to be loaded on the bark *Seminole* and transported to southeast Alaska. From there they were to go overland to Dyea, across the

Chilcoot Pass, and into the Klondike region with relief supplies. Jackson himself went directly to Washington from New York, under the impression that his part had been accomplished, only to hear that the emergency situation had ended. He was ordered to go to Seattle immediately and salvage whatever he could of the project, distributing the reindeer to various stations in Alaska and locating the herdsmen where they could do the most good.

At Seattle he discovered that the *Seminole* had not reached port and that the moss brought from Europe for the reindeer was almost gone. The vessel was nine days overdue by the time it arrived. In the meantime, substitute fodder had been purchased for the herd. The change in diet killed about a dozen animals and sickened many more. Further trouble would have been averted if there had not also been a delay in transmitting orders for Alaskan moss through Army channels. Jackson's plan was to land the animals at Haines Station in southeast Alaska and give them a chance to regain their strength on moss brought in from nearby. But instructions sent to the commanding officer at Dyea from Skagway five miles away took a week to reach their destination; the moss, therefore, was not on hand when the reindeer arrived. Even the tents and other equipment for the drivers and their families did not arrive on time. Jackson then tried to drive the herd to moss beds a short distance from Haines, but they were so weak that the Lapps advised him to abandon the plan and keep the herd at Haines while moss was collected and brought to them.

The weakened, starving herd grew smaller each day. Three or four animals died every twenty-four hours. Many more were in such poor condition that when the moss was brought to the station, they were unable to digest it. By the time the herd was able to travel, half the animals were dead. To make matters worse, many more died the following weeks. This situation would have produced criticism even under the most favorable circumstances, but in light of the fact that the animals were not needed for relief work, the attacks upon those who had any part in the project were especially bitter. Eventually the animals were distributed and the herdsmen taken to various stations in Alaska. Jackson left Alaska on April 8, having done all that was humanly possible. He arrived back in Washington on the twenty-third of the month, very unhappy with what had happened but powerless to do more than make a report of the facts.

CHAPTER 11

JOURNEY TO KAMCHATKA

There were many indications that Jackson's boundless energies and unflagging spirits were diminishing when he returned to Alaska in the summer of 1898. In the course of his life he had endured physical hardships that would have appalled a younger man. His emotional reserves had been seriously depleted by the constant bickering and criticism of his administration of the schools. No matter how much evidence existed to support his wisdom in starting the reindeer project, there were still opponents who denied any merit in the work. There are also intimations in his correspondence of this period that some of those in the territory upon whom he had to depend were not always as completely loyal to him as he would have been to them. Professional jealousies, second-guessing, and misjudged motives formed a shadowy background to the open attacks leveled against him. In spite of all this, Jackson made every effort to hide the signs of his fatigue and illness by remaining on the job—not so much out of plain stubbornness as from a deep concern for people who needed help. Whatever else one might say of him, those who knew him intimately saw a gentleness and patience not always apparent to others. It is interesting, too, that one of his close associates described him as a person who never hurried, only persisted.

Persistence carried him over sixty thousand miles in less than one year: up the Yukon River valley to Dawson City and along the coast of the Bering Sea during the latter half of 1897, the trip to Lapland and return at the start of 1898, the return trip to Alaska to pick up the pieces when the reindeer expedition fell apart. There is virtually nothing in his journals for this period to indicate that he was suffering great pain, although there is other evidence that he was seldom free of suffering. Nor are there other complaints about his difficulties. He was approaching the end of his career as the nineteenth century drew to a close, but he was doing it in the manner in which he had started—without regard for the cost to himself and without extolling his own virtues.

The trip to Alaska in 1898 made one fact quite clear: if additional reindeer were to be strategically placed it would have to be done soon. But inasmuch as there were few prospects of buying animals from natives who had already sold to him, he concluded that the next best place to visit was the Kamchatka Peninsula, farther south on the Siberian coast. Since there was no opportunity to go there in 1898, plans were laid to make the trip in 1899. Jackson's notes for that period reveal the ever-changing focus of an intensely alert mind, responsive to large and small details, probing and analyzing every event and condition. The *Bear* was not ready to put to sea when he reached Seattle, so he made use of the delay to take a trip to Tacoma. There he spoke to the city Board of Trade about Alaska's potential and the reindeer work. He also addressed a group of teachers on schools problems in Alaska and the need for more courses in manual training and animal husbandry. He gave another talk before the Alaska Geographical Society at Washington State University. When he returned to Seattle and found that the *Bear* was still not ready to leave, he accepted an invitation to discuss

Seattle's trade relations with the territory before the Seattle Chamber of Commerce.

Under way at last, the *Bear* stopped at Port Townsend after leaving Seattle and gave Jackson an opportunity to walk around the town. He noted that "empty stores everywhere testify to the greatness of the collapse from boom times."

Once the revenue steamer had left the States, it made good progress toward the Aleutians, reaching the vicinity of Unalaska in the first week of June. Passing close to Akutan, Jackson had a very good view of the volcano, for it stood out "clear and cold, covered with an unusual amount of snow. The crater was not at the highest point, but upon the eastern shoulder of the mountain, and was plainly marked by the large black spot on the snow-covered mountain, made by the snow being melted away from the rocks that form the rim of the crater. On the west shoulder of the volcano a large pile of perpendicular rocks forming a small mountain of themselves, covered sides and tops with snow and ice glistening in the sun. [It] seemed like a gigantic fairy ice palace . . . further heightened by some bare rocks at the base, giving the appearance of a large arched doorway. At the mouth of the pass for a short time the tide rips made a rough sea causing the vessel to roll badly."

The revenue ship crossed into Russian waters, entered Avacha Bay, and headed for Petropavlovsk, the capital of the Kamchatka Peninsula. Jackson was thrilled by the great mountain range that came down to the coast, enclosing Avacha Bay like "some gigantic amphitheatre concealed behind the curtain of fog . . . precipices walling into the waters and great columns rising out of the sea like eternal sentinels. . . ." As soon as the *Bear* anchored off Petropavlovsk, Jackson and Healy paid a courtesy call on the Russian governor, or *ispravnik*, and presented their credentials, which included a letter from the Russian ambassador in Washington.

Later in the day, while climbing to the top of a ridge overlooking the village for a better view of the mountains, Jackson found two memorials. One was a cenotaph to Vitus Bering, whose stubborn search of northern waters laid the foundation for Russia's claim to Alaska. The other was a monument to a French explorer, Jean François de Galaup, Comte de la Pérouse, whose exploits excited Jackson's imagination. More than a hundred years before, he had sailed into Avacha Bay and been seen for the last time on earth near Petropavlovsk. Setting out from Brest in the summer of 1785, La Pérouse, like Franklin and others, had gone in search of a northwest passage linking Europe and Asia. A year later he was in the South Pacific to determine whaling possibilities. He sailed north toward southeast Alaska until bad weather drove his two ships southwest to the Hawaiian Islands, then farther west to Macao, the Philippines, and the coasts of Korea and Japan. Almost two years from the day he left France, La Pérouse was off Vladivostok, heading through the strait that separates Sakhalin from the northernmost island of Japan—a strait which still bears his name on some maps. He dropped anchor at Petropavlovsk so that one of his officers could travel overland to Paris with charts and maps of the oceans they had crossed and the lands they had visited. A few days later they sailed out of Avacha. Almost forty years passed before the world knew anything about the fate of La Pérouse and the crews of his two ships; the wreckage found on the shore of an island in the New Hebrides group told the story.

Jackson never thought of himself as either explorer or adventurer, yet he had a kinship with all who were. He understood the courage that was required for a man to pursue a goal across unmarked waters to unknown lands and the need for an inner conviction of the rightness of one's efforts. In whatever role he cast himself and however others saw him, he too possessed the doggedness of men like Bering and La Pérouse.

Petropavlovsk had a history of its own in addition to the place it held in the La Pérouse story. A combined French and English fleet had bombarded the village during the Crimean War after failing to trap the Russian Imperial Navy in the harbor. But when they tried to storm the settlement, Russian sharpshooters cut the attackers to pieces and drove survivors over a cliff. After the fleet withdrew, the Russians abandoned Petropavlovsk, first destroying everything of value. They returned in 1856 and rebuilt the village. They also buried the allied casualties next to their own dead in a tiny cemetery outside the settlement.

History, however, was not the reason that brought Jackson to Kamchatka. As soon as he realized that the visit to Petropavlovsk was going to be unproductive, he and Healy decided to head north to the mouth of the Kamchatka River so that he could try his luck buying reindeer at a village three miles inland. It was a useless effort. There were herds in the interior, but none of the villagers would seek out their owners for Jackson.

The Fourth of July on Kamchatka was a damp and chilly affair. The mercury did not rise above fifty-six degrees the entire day. Healy fired a twenty-one-gun salute that echoed and re-echoed against the coastal range, probably scaring away any herders who might have ventured to the shore. The noise did not frighten one native who signaled to the *Bear* a couple of days later; Jackson went ashore in haste lest the man change his mind and disappear with his animals. Fifty-three head were taken on board that same day. The following morning another herder arrived and sold sixty-three more head. The animals varied in cost depending on their size, age, and health. Those in the poorest condition sold for two dollars and twenty-five cents; the best were valued at four dollars and eighty-five cents each. Jackson's carefully kept accounts of his reindeer transactions provide information about the prices of certain items at the turn of the century. Fifty yards of calico cost three dollars. Ten cakes of tea, two dollars and ten cents. A copper kettle, three and a quarter. Ten pounds of sugar, forty-five cents. Fifteen sacks of flour (apparently fifty-pound sacks) cost twelve dollars. A .44 caliber Winchester rifle, ten dollars and twenty-eight cents. A Winchester described as a .45-.70 sold for sixteen dollars and twenty cents.

In the light of later claims that Jackson mismanaged appropriations and the suggestion that he turned some of the funds to his own purposes, it is interesting to note what painstaking records he made, even to the point of listing the purchase price of one group of animals at two dollars and twenty-five and one-third cents. Every bar of soap, every extra meal for an interpreter was also listed. He might have been excused for omitting details about goods sold to a mission station in need of supplies, but every such transaction is listed and the individual prices quoted. Furthermore, anyone who planned to convert funds to his own use would have had a hard time making much on the relatively few dollars provided for either the reindeer or the schools.

The *Bear* was back in American waters by Wednesday, July 12, when she stopped at Gambell on St. Lawrence Island to pick up two missionaries who had finished their tour of duty. One of the men, also in the government teaching service, reported that a drunken native had tried to murder him. On the basis of information supplied by the missionaries, Healy sent a shore patrol back to Gambell to arrest the captain of a whaling ship, who was charged with selling whiskey to the natives. The man was placed in irons until he could be turned over to the nearest United States commissioner for trial.

The revenue steamer then headed straight for Point Rodney because six fawn included among Jackson's last purchase had died and there was fear for the safety of the remaining animals. But the sea was running so high at Rodney that Healy had to sail for Port Clarence where, in spite of continuing heavy surf, it seemed wiser to risk losing the cargo in trying to get it ashore than to keep the animals penned on the steamer.

One of the limitations on the buying of reindeer was that July and August were the only months when the weather was fairly consistent and the sea relatively free of ice. As a consequence, Healy had to fit the trips to Siberia between calls at points in the possession, which accounts for a large share of his shuttling back and forth between Siberian and American waters. On occasions the revenue cutter service was able to spare a second ship to assist Jackson and take some of the work load from Healy, but no one could ever depend on that. To ensure the best possible use of the open season, Jackson authorized the captains of several commercial ships to transact business with the Siberian natives on his behalf and provided the captains with barter goods. This arrangement often worked well, but in 1899 he discovered that one of his captains had double-crossed him. The man had sold most of the goods given to him for trading and used the proceeds to put himself into the mercantile business. He hoped to make a financial killing with the discovery of the Nome placer gold deposits. A small part of the goods he had traded for cheap whiskey to use in buying reindeer in Siberia, with the usual bad aftereffects. Jackson's comment on the case was that it illustrated the "failings and shortcomings of employees." He deplored what he termed the "unjust and malicious assertions and reports of captains of whalers and others who, from their position and dangerous occupation, ought to take a special interest in the stocking of the frozen north with domestic herds . . . the great difficulty of procuring reindeer in Siberia altogether makes the work one of great discouragement and perplexity." He could never understand why people looked upon his efforts as beneficial only to the natives, for he thought of his work in terms of the total life of Alaska. If he was ever hurt by the attitude of others, it was when they failed to credit him with doing his best under the worst conditions. The attitude of Major General A. W. Greely, the United States Army officer who had criticized the Klondike relief expedition as a waste of time and money, makes sense. Greely wrote that "doubtless in [the reindeer work], as in other novel and extended enterprises, there were errors in administration and policy, with exaggerated and consequent disappointments, but, as a whole, the policy was wise and the results valuable and far-reaching . . . as a body the representatives of the various churches in Alaska are devoted, self-sacrificing men and women, who labor faithfully and strenuously for the welfare of the natives, often under the most discouraging and trying circumstances."

There was one group in Alaska for whom Jackson was not able to do very much, but for that matter no one could. They were the forsaken, gold-hungry men who flocked from one part of the territory to another in search of riches. They chased each rainbow to where it touched the earth, only to find that others had gotten there first and seized the treasure. More often than not they discovered the treasure was not half of what it had been reported to be. Again and again at the first faint glimmer of new prospects of wealth, they would take off with fresh hope, a bedraggled lot, many of them living on dreams drenched in the sweat of back-breaking labor. These were the unhonored partners of Alaska's miseries; not all the cadence of poetry nor the drama of romance has ever caught the full depth of their anguish.

Jackson was on the final leg of his journey in 1899 when he found himself in the midst of one chapter of the gold frenzy. The *Bear* was on her way south from Cape Prince of Wales when she overtook a heavy-laden schooner, crowded with miners who were fleeing the worked-out Kotzebue mining district. Healy suspected that the schooner was a ship that had been stolen at St. Michael and sailed to Kotzebue by a group of prospectors who had heard reports that gold had been discovered there in great quantities. As the revenue boat came abeam of the shooner, Healy's suspicions were confirmed. He sent a boarding party with orders that the captain of the schooner be brought back to the *Bear*. Faced by Healy with evidence that the schooner was not his, the man broke down and admitted taking the vessel. He also described living conditions at Kotzebue, painting such a dark picture that Healy felt he had to make an investigation of the area. The moment the *Bear* reached Cape Blossom it was apparent that the captain of the schooner had understated the situation. Whatever gold there was had been worked out quickly, leaving between three hundred and fifty to four hundred miners penniless without any means of subsistence or of transportation. Most of them were in extremely poor physical condition. Healy could make no more than the vaguest estimate of the number who had already died from disease, starvation, drowning, subzero weather, or violence. Among many the hope of recovery was so weak that it could never be revived. To add to their miseries, hordes of mosquitoes descended upon them day and night. Thirty-three of the worst cases were taken to the *Bear* for emergency treatment and transportation to settlements where they could receive proper care. Another party from the steamer found forty-eight others, including two women and a baby, who were so debilitated that Healy could not leave them behind. As the *Bear* left the area, it was like turning one's back on men doomed to a bitter and lingering death.

The revenue steamer overtook the schooner once more and ordered it to Anvil City near Cape Nome since its passengers wanted to go there. It seemed more sensible to take them there than to dump them on shore at St. Michael and add to that community's problems. Anvil City was a city in name only, typical of the many settlements that sprang up overnight wherever gold was discovered. It was located at the mouth of the Snake River on Norton Sound, a motley collection of tents and shanties stretching about twenty miles along each side of the river, plus a few houses and a couple of warehouses. Prospectors panned for gold everywhere, some of them working in the very center of the settlement. No one at Anvil City now known as Nome, worried too much about the future; each man was convinced that he would strike it rich before the end came. This was a symptom of the gold fever: the present was the only time that mattered. If they had not rejected the past so completely, many of the miners at Anvil City would have remembered St. Michael across the sound and lost their enthusiasm. St. Michael had been bursting at the seams with men and activity a year earlier as miners sought passage up the Yukon to the Klondike. Merchants did a thriving business. A year later the town was still filled with men, but they were headed away from the Klondike, filled with disgust or angry because they had not had a chance to try their luck in the gold fields. With the last of the miners gone, the town returned to comparative oblivion.

Jackson himself was bitten a little by the gold bug in 1899. He and several men, including Lopp at Cape Prince of Wales, formed a mining district in Lopp's vicinity. While he was at Nome, Jackson gave a lawyer there the power of attorney to locate several placer mines in his name. In the absence of any evidence to the contrary, he appears to have been no more successful than hundreds of others.

Jackson transferred to the revenue steamer *Thetis* after visiting the Nome area, so that he might make another quick trip to Siberia. He bought forty head and landed them at Lopp's station, then went south to wrap up the odds and ends of the season's activities. He picked up a bundle of furs trapped by a missionary, intending to sell them for the man where he could get the best price. He stopped at the Swedish Evangelical and Moravian mission stations to check the condition of their buildings so that repair work could be planned for 1900. He visited the Lapp herders whom he had brought to Alaska, paid them their salaries, and satisfied himself as to their health and welfare. He also made arrangements with the Swedish mission at Golovin Bay for establishing a herd there the following year. At Gambell he opened a new mission. The next stop was Dutch Harbor for an inspection of the government and contract schools. He discovered that the school work had lapsed because the teacher assigned to the Methodist mission had not arrived. The school at Unga was also closed for the same reason. The *Thetis* ran into a succession of bad storms and Jackson was sick for several days. He had recovered sufficiently by the time the ship reached Yakutat to investigate the effects of earthquakes that had rocked the region. Several mission buildings had been damaged, but none of the personnel was hurt. From Yakutat, he went to Sitka to join Governor Brady for a tour of government and contract schools at Juneau, Wrangell, Ketchikan, Metlakatla, and Saxman. Then he left for Washington, D.C., stopping en route at Salt Lake City, which was a point of special interest for him.

After years of planning, he had helped to found Westminster College there in the spring of 1895. Jackson continued as the guardian angel of the college for several years, providing funds for new construction and for the salary of the president.

The first news to reach Jackson when he arrived in Washington on October 13 was that a new storm had broken over his head, a repetition of old attacks and familiar charges that he had been mismanaging government funds. The latest assault developed from another Sitka grand jury, whose foreman was the former governor, A. P. Swineford. As on a previous occasion, it was charged that Jackson had falsified progress reports on the school system. Jeannette Nichols is of the opinion that "the deplorable lack of school facilities in southeast Alaska, the infrequent visit of the agent and the comparatively munificent government expenditures for reindeer, gave considerable color to the charges." At the same time, she characterizes Jackson as an "impractical enthusiast, by nature lacking in business ability." She prefaces these unqualified statements with the remark that "a careful investigation of the attacks upon Doctor Jackson at various times in his career fails to justify the charge that he personally profited from the misuse of government funds, although some of his transactions . . . might have sent a less influential man to jail."

For the most part, the 1899 charges were a repetition of the allegations made in 1885 and in 1896. Former Alaska governor James Sheakley held his own opinion of the charges. He pointed out that Jackson never handled cash in his official capacity and that he used vouchers which had to pass the scrutiny of other federal officials in the territory. The logic of Sheakley's point is quite clear: if there had ever been any concrete evidence of misuse of funds, Jackson's opponents would have cited the facts. In addition, any such misuse of government funds would have required the connivance of others who held office in Alaska, but no one ever claimed that Jackson was in league with others to defraud the government. Possibly it is difficult to get a clear-cut picture of Jackson's administrative problems because people were either completely for or completely against him. The United States Commissioner for Education in 1899, W. T. Harris, who had no reason other than evidence to support him against the charges, made it very clear that in his opinion the charges had no substance in fact. Harris also wrote a letter to an officer in the revenue service who had come to Jackson's defense, thanking him for his assistance. "For ten years I have heard complaints of all kinds against [Jackson]," Harris wrote, "but I have never in any case found that the charges would bear investigating . . . he is a man of the highest integrity and honest in his dealings with his fellow men."

The naturalist and paleontologist William H. Dall, who spent years in the territory, observed that Jackson's relations with the white population of Alaska were complicated by the "ability, fidelity, and energy with which [Jackson] sought to serve the purpose of the government and his sharpness and persistence in exposing the misconduct of those who would impose on the ignorance" of others.

A friend once told Jackson that he would have to "look beyond this world for a sufficient reward for [your] services." He never felt that he had to find justification in the eyes of the world, for when a person believes as firmly as did Jackson that he must answer to only one Master, his inner self is buttressed against attack.

He made his last inspection trip to the Arctic in 1900. Though he had an assistant to help him by then, he was determined to remain as active as possible. But sixteen thousand miles of travel, most of it under extremely trying conditions, was not the kind of diet upon which a man of sixty-six could thrive. This time he was less able to throw off the effects of illness and the long absences from home. He wrote one sentence in his diary that is indicative of his state of mind: "Felt lonesome and blue this evening." Thereafter the Arctic region became the responsibility of an assistant. Jackson remained on the job, however, confining his trips in 1901 and 1902 to an inspection of schools and reindeer stations along the Bering coast and in the southeast. He planned another trip to Alaska in 1903, but illness forced him to cancel it and remain in the United States on the advice of his physician.

CHAPTER 12

UNDER FIRE TO THE END

One of Jackson's longest personal associations in Alaska was with John Brady, the former Presbyterian missionary who had gone into business in the territory and later served as its governor from 1897-1906. Their relationship had advantages for Jackson as well as drawbacks. In the matter of principles and general objectives—particularly in the establishment of schools and missions for the natives—the two men saw eye to eye. They differed, to a greater or less degree, over the best means for developing Alaska politically and were at variance over the question of keeping prohibition on the law books. Brady felt that a licensing system would be a more effective means of controlling the liquor traffic and at the same time producing needed revenue for the territory. On most matters they worked together in the interest of creating a morally strong, sound, and productive community. The fact that Brady was a churchman who adhered to his principles provided a bond with Jackson that was indestructible.

Another link between them was that one or the other was under constant attack, usually from the same groups and for the same reasons. They were often accused of hampering the development of Alaska. Brady, according to Nichols, was charged with "narrow-mindedness and inability" by a "great many honest Alaskans who were not interested in politics" but who "seconded the opposition to [him]," although admitting that he would have been a suitable governor about 1889. No one in Alaska seems to have had any doubt about his honesty, but he antagonized many because, among other matters, he refused to support a proposal to move the capital from Sitka to Juneau. He believed that Alaska should remain unorganized until it was ready for statehood in view of the small numbers and poor quality of its population. From the standpoint of practical politics, Brady's opinions and activities contributed to some of the confusion existing in Washington over what was best for Alaska and handicapped the efforts of those who sought greater home rule. Nichols feels that he "suffered greatly from his impractical unworldliness and failure to follow a policy agreeable to the business people," although she says that "a more conservative faction . . . was inclined to absolve Jackson and Brady of part of the blame for Alaska's ills."

There was no question in Jackson's mind about Brady's value as Alaska's governor, for when his name was up for reappointment in 1904, Jackson wrote a very pointed letter which he circulated among influential people in Washington:

The appointment of the Reverend John G. Brady, Governor of Alaska, terminates on the sixth of June. In the whole history of Alaska it has had but two good governors, [James Sheakley] a Democratic appointee by Mr. Cleveland on his second term, and [Brady] appointed by Mr. McKinley just previous to his death.

The friends of good order and the substantial property holders of Alaska are in favor of Governor Brady's reappointment. His opponents are men who stand for measures which we deem pernicious and which he had persistently fought.

If you are willing to help us in Alaska to good government, will you not write President Roosevelt and ask that Mr. Brady be continued Governor because of the good, faithful, honest, and efficient services already rendered in that position. Please do not use my name in writing to him.

Very truly yours,
Sheldon Jackson,
General Agent of Education in Alaska

Nichols observed that "judging from the newspaper comment [the reappointment of Brady in 1904] was not expected [in Alaska], but it was readily explained as an evidence of the continued control of Alaska policy by the Presbyterian Board of Home Missions which was so powerful that the party leaders were unwilling to oppose it. . . ." There can be serious argument over the extent to which "Alaska policy" was controlled by the board, for if the board had had its way there would have been far more enforcement of law than there was. It would be more accurate to speak of Jackson's continued control of "Alaska policy," but here again it is difficult to reconcile such alleged control with the vast areas in which Jackson was unable to get the action he desired. Assuming, however, that it is correct to speak of the mission board's control over "Alaska policy," that power declined sufficiently between 1904 and 1906 for President Roosevelt to feel that he could remove Brady without fear of the consequences—if the fear of the influence of the Church ever existed to the degree that was claimed.

If the Presbyterian Board of Home Missions did exert tremendous pressure on the administration, it was not alone in doing so, although it was certainly distinguished by the kind of persuasion it brought to bear and the objectives it sought. All the large Alaskan commercial interests maintained lobbies of one kind or another in the nation's capital. The Alaska Commercial Company, blamed by Swineford and others for the lack of effective government in the territory, was one such group. Others were the North American Transportation and

Trading Company, which operated steamers on the Yukon together with the ACC; the Alaska Packers Association, the North American Commercial Company, the Treadwell Mining Company, and the Pacific Steamer Whaler Company. Each one had its particular interest—the Yukon Valley trade, fisheries, seals, whales, and general mercantile interests.

If the Church had its Jacksons and Bradys, companies like the Alaska Commercial Company, to select just one, had their protectors. Among the ACC officers and individuals interested in the company were men like John F. Miller, who had been a United States Senator and a former Collector of Customs in San Francisco. There was also O. P. Morton, another former United States Senator; former congressman T. D. Eliot; and H. H. McIntyre, formerly special commissioner for the United States Treasury Department in Alaska. These men were interested in making a financial success out of the Alaska Commercial Company, and it is not assuming too much to believe that their humanitarian impulses toward the territory were far less than their concern for extracting from it as many dollars as possible with the least amount of interference from Alaskans, Congress, or the administration in Washington.

Brady was reappointed governor in time to come under the shadow of the final indictment of Jackson's work as general agent for education. The resentment of Alaskans was erupting with increasing violence and frequency as years went by without an appreciable improvement in their status. The turn of the century saw greatly increased demands for changes in federal personnel and the appointment of Alaskan residents to positions of importance in the territory. The long list of economic grievances which became a little longer with each passing year, formed the backbone of the complaints reaching Washington. The furor reached such a peak that President

Roosevelt asked the Department of the Interior to send one of its men to Alaska to report on the "condition of educational and school service and the management of reindeer service." Frank C. Churchill got the assignment.

Churchill went to Alaska in the summer of 1905, spent three months at sea sailing from one place to another, and was back in Washington, submitting his report, in December 1905. He added three supplementary statements in 1906.

He questioned the manner of handling funds appropriated by Congress for the reindeer work and the general management of the project. He assailed the practice of lending herds to Lapp and Norwegian herders as not being in the government's interest. He was particularly disturbed about the placement of herds at mission stations, implying that Jackson did this to enable the missions to develop at government expense. He further claimed that Jackson did not list receipts and disbursements clearly and questioned whether Bureau of Education reports on schools and reindeer were complete. He spoke of an "air of mystery around the administration of the Bureau's affairs [in Alaska] not altogether desirable"; argued that "when those of [Jackson's] own church were placed on the government payroll it is not strange" that sectarian jealousies arise.

Churchill also referred to the fact that Jackson received support from the Presbyterian Board of Home Missions in addition to his salary as a government official, the suggestion being that Jackson was thus influenced to favor the Church. And concerning the money that Jackson raised privately to inaugurate the reindeer work, Churchill said "it has been intimated . . . that this contribution has furnished excuse for giving away thousands of dollars worth of government property. . . ."

As for the missionaries, he felt that they were not equipped to "cover all the needs" of the Eskimos. As for the schools, he said, "I know of no adverse criticism that should be made as to the quality of service rendered by the teachers employed."

In a brief conclusion to his report, Churchill urged an end to lending deer to individuals or groups without prior approval of the Secretary of the Interior; proposed closer supervision over the schools and reindeer work with a supervisor at Nome; suggested monthly and quarterly reports in triplicate; the management and control of the schools and reindeer to be within the Department of the Interior proper; placement of all schools outside incorporated towns under control of the Secretary of the Interior; and "so far as practicable, only such persons as are skilled in medicine should be employed as teachers in the arctic and sub-arctic."

Whatever may be said for or against Churchill's assessment of Alaska's woes, the fact remains that he made no serious effort to judge whether the evidence he had received in support of the complaints was fair and accurate and whether the data he had been given could be sustained as fact. It is difficult otherwise to understand how his report could have been so negative. Its major effect was to provide old fuel for an old fire. The implication that the federal government had been defrauded deliberately provided a rallying point for patriots anxious to demonstrate their zeal. Even in the face of the most distorted claims, it is strange that Churchill did not examine the official records. Had he done so, he could hardly have reported that the denominational missions were the only ones to benefit from the government's reindeer project, leaving the natives no better off than before. At the same time that this report was submitted, a number of newspaper stories appeared, re-emphasizing the charge that the natives had derived no benefit from the importation of animals from Siberia. These accounts opened the way to additional personal slurs on Jackson, one of the sharpest of which appeared in the

New York *Herald*. Anyone who knew the slightest bit about him could have understood that every claim of fraud was ludicrous.

As a whole, the report bears many evidences of superficiality, and while Churchill denied imputing fraudulent practices it is easy enough to assume malpractice from what he says. In support of his remark about the air of mystery that surrounded Jackson's administration, he cites as an exhibit a letter from one Harry P. Corser, who identified himself as "pastor of the People's Church" at Wrangell, and a former Presbyterian missionary who was "dropped out of the Church" after criticizing Jackson. The letter proves little if anything. There were those who felt that the report was a rehash of long-standing differences between Jackson and one of his subordinates in the reindeer work in Alaska. As for the money Jackson received from the Board of Home Missions, that was a fact that had been acknowledged by the Bureau of Education and a situation that it desired since it could not increase Jackson's government salary. The Commissioner of Education, W. T. Harris, commented after studying the report that "the official records are sufficient to show the slender basis of the popular criticisms in the report." He went on to say that the report was "incomplete . . . in that it does not place the fragments of facts together with the facts in their entirety as found in official reports from Alaska or as would have been found from a more thorough investigation on the ground than Mr. Churchill's time permitted."

The accusations against Jackson were not pushed so much for the purpose of instigating criminal action against him as to effect his removal, to eliminate his close associates such as Brady, and to blunt the influence of the Church—all for the purpose of freeing Alaska of moral strictures. Many persons had come to the conclusion, some of them hesitantly, that the churches were a dead weight and a dampening influence politically. In this climate the enemies of the church groups thrived. Others in and out of government, however, came to Jackson's support, and United States Commissioner of Education Harris challenged the accuracy of the Churchill conclusions.

The facts in the reindeer work provided a picture quite different from that painted by the President's representative. One thousand two hundred and eighty reindeer were brought to Alaska between 1891 and 1906, exclusive of the two years when the Russian government forbade their export. By the end of 1905, about the time that Churchill was putting his findings together, there were 12,828, including the 10,548 born in the territory. The United States government spent a total of $122,500 on the project from 1893 to 1905, Jackson having raised funds privately for the work in 1891 and 1892. Fifteen new reindeer stations had been opened between 1899 and 1906. One year prior to the Churchill report, there were seventy-eight native apprentices in Alaska who owned 38 per cent of all the herds. During the same period, the federal government owned 30 per cent, the mission stations held 21 per cent, and the Lapps—under the terms of their government contracts—had 11 per cent of the herds. By 1906 native apprentices owned about seven thousand animals or more than half of the total number. Four hundred and seventy-five animals had been broken to harness by then for commercial transportation purposes.

The number of reindeer herds rose to forty-seven by 1912 and were centered around twenty-eight stations, eighteen of them government owned and the remaining ten related to mission stations. The number of animals increased to ninety-five thousand in 1917 with about the same proportion in native hands as in 1906. The reindeer population reached its highest point in 1936 when the figure stood at about six hundred thousand, but increased butchering, loss of winter ranges because of overgrazing, depredation by wolves, and mixing with wild caribou reduced the number until the herds totaled about twenty-five thousand head in 1950, more than half of which were owned by natives.

As is often the case with controversies that exist more because of personal antipathies than for any other reason, emotions rather than facts prevailed in the last stages of the reindeer-Jackson dispute. Jackson tried to explain in January 1906 that the government's policy in lending animals was to the advantage both of the government and of the natives. The key to the program's success was that the missions bore the expense of caring for the herds and training the native apprentices.

The herds located at Point Barrow, Gambell on St. Lawrence Island, Bettles, and Iliamna belonged to the government in 1906 and Washington paid all costs. The herds at Deering (a Friends mission) were cared for by two Eskimo herders who were paid a total of four hundred dollars a year. The Roman Catholic mission at Holy Cross had a Lapp herder who was paid five hundred dollars a year. These two missions also paid all the other expenses in connection with their apprentice training program. The herds located at Kivalina, Kotzebue, Shishmaref, Wales, Teller, Golovin, Unalakleet, and Bethel were maintained without expense to the government.

One man who was in an excellent position to evaluate the reindeer project was Clarence L. Andrews. He was at Teller after the first reindeer were landed in Alaska and served from 1923 to 1929 in the School and Reindeer Service. Andrews wrote in 1939 that he "counted [the reindeer project] the greatest and most practicable plan ever put into practise for the well-being of a native people of the United States."

It is only fair to point out that there are those who believe that while the reindeer project served an immediate need, its long-term value to the Eskimos is questionable; that the money spent to introduce the reindeer, develop the herds, and train native herders could have been spent more profitably in teaching handicraft trades and skills to the Eskimos.

The section of the Churchill report that dealt with the schools was also deficient in that it made use of none of the facts known at the time, the most obvious being, as everyone agreed in one way or another, that Congress had never provided sufficient funds. The federal government's annual school appropriation was fifty thousand dollars during most of the years Jackson was general agent for education. How much more was needed can be seen from the fact that the Presbyterian Board of Home Missions spent thirty-four thousand dollars on the Point Barrow mission and school alone from 1890 to 1905. But Churchill was alleging that during this same period the government had provided nearly all the funds expended at Barrow on behalf of the natives. The Presbyterians spent thousands of dollars at other mission schools, while other denominations contributed comparable sums.

Earlier population figures for Alaska seem at variance with one another due in part to the lack of good census facilities, but by 1900—when the figures were fairly accurate—the territory's white population was 34,056 as compared with 29,536 natives. Although one cannot say with certainty how many of the whites were single men, it is evident that they represented a large percentage of the total. The native population, on the other hand, was family-based for the most part. Hence by 1900 the native population of school age was far in excess of the white. Furthermore, as Gruening points out, there were about one hundred and seventy-seven native villages with a school population totaling four thousand which were still without schools in 1905. He adds that "twenty years after the federal government had assumed responsibility [for educational facilities] at least three-quarters of the native children were without schooling." The Alaskan delegate to Congress claimed in 1933 that the Indians in the territory had received only one third as much "federal aid of any kind" as the Indians in the States. And certainly no one could argue that the American Indian was pampered. Yet in spite of all this, it was still being claimed when Churchill made his report that the natives were receiving a disproportionate share of school funds.

One can understand that the parents of white children were not concerned with comparative statistics, except insofar as they supported their contention that white children were discriminated against in favor of the natives. Most signs point to the fact that the white Alaskans were interested in preferred, rather than relatively equal treatment. That would appear to be a fair interpretation of their constant complaints. Nichols insists that as the lot of the native improved, the "white grew all the more conscious of his own woes and disabilities," certainly a natural result of all the hardships Alaskans had to endure.

It would have been helpful if the Churchill report had underscored other factors which bore heavily on the effective functioning of Alaska's school system, quite apart from its administration: the great distance between the territory and its administrative center in Washington, the distances between schools within the possession and the lack of good transportation facilities, and sectional jealousies (the fears of the people in Skagway and Juneau, for example, that Sitka was getting the lion's share of available funds, and vice versa). The criticism upon which all Alaskans were united was that the federal government refused to give local communities the authority or the means to participate in the school work. Few seemed to recall that when local participation had been tried it had proved unsuccessful.

Nichols is consistently critical of the school system. She says that "to cap the climax, in 1893, constitutional objections and sectarian rivalry put a stop to the much-abused government subsidy of mission schools." It is difficult, in the light of other testimony, to validate her use of the words "much-abused." The opinion should, however, be recorded because it is possible that the appearance of abuse grew out of the zeal with which the missionaries went about their tasks and the emphasis they placed on educating the natives. Nichols also speaks, in reference to the school complaints in 1899 which provided a background for the Churchill claims, of "the deplorable lack of school facilities in southeast Alaska, the infrequent visits of the agent and the comparatively munificent government expenditures for reindeer [which] gave considerable color to the charges. . . ."

Alaskans finally received some voice in local school matters in 1900. The passage of the civil code in that year provided that 50 per cent of all revenue collected in the territory could be returned to local communities for educational purposes. The code also provided for municipal and district schools, but, according to Gruening, it was not until 1917 that the "foundations of a comprehensive public-school system were laid . . . fifty years after Alaska had come under the American flag." This places the responsibility for the state of Alaskan education where it belongs: on the federal government and on Congress in particular. Alaskans paid a big price for being Americans.

Chief Justice of the United States Court of Claims Stanton J. Peele made the following evaluation of the charges against his friend Jackson contained in the Churchill report:

". . . while honest and well meaning men are liable to make mistakes both in theory and practice, I am sure that when the purpose and management of both . . . are known, it will be conceded that behind it all have been faithful, conscientious men who were guided by prayerful consideration, whose conviction to public duty will repel any charge of neglect. . . .

". . . No doubt designing white men who want to speculate off the reindeer and reap all the profit therefore possible, including the food so bountifully supplied by the government free from cost, are busy spreading rumors detrimental to the policy of the Bureau [of Education]. . . ."

Evidently there were enough persons in Congress who felt as Peele did, for the legislature did not act on any of the suggestions contained in the report for revamping the procedures of the Department of the Interior and its Office of Education as administered by Jackson. True, congressional failure to act may not have been the best vindication of Jackson's work; more than likely, continued disinterest in Alaskan affairs obviated any thoughtful consideration of the report. But, when one considers Congress' attitude in the light of the facts involved, it is apparent that no one thought there were any very serious conditions that needed to be rectified.

Governor Brady's removal from office by President Roosevelt was the one principal result of the Churchill report, and that may have been done as much for political reasons as for any other. Brady's own comment upon passing from the official scene was that he welcomed the opportunity to get his family out of Sitka so as "to obtain better educational facilities"—an indictment of the parsimonious attitude displayed by Congress toward Alaska's schools. Brady also commented on another problem with which Jackson was familiar: the extent of prejudice among white people against the natives, especially in the churches. Brady wrote to Jackson that he and his family would "like to live in a Christian community for a while. Right now we are in the midst of contentions in this little town [Sitka] that make us heartsick. The one thing wanting in it all is Christian charity. In fact, we are more truly heathen than the natives."

Brady was not being spiteful when he touched this Achilles' heel of the Church. There were congregational difficulties and failures in keeping Christian practice on as high a level as Christian faith. None of this was lost upon those who felt that church people were not all they claimed to be; hardheaded business interests took a particularly jaundiced view of such shortcomings. This hypocritical attitude among church people contributed much to what has been described as a changing of the old order in Alaska and its yielding place to the new. Nichols' comment with respect to one denomination was probably true of the Church as a whole in the territory:

"The Presbyterian Church had exercised an influence second only to that of the commercial companies during a quarter of a century . . . but during the last decade Alaska had become a country of white prospectors, geological experts, partisan politicians, and investment companies, with which the Church had no points of contact; so it slipped down and out. . . ."

It was, actually, not that simple. The Church, with Jackson as its outstanding representative, was caught between two forces. One was the bitter, often cynical and despairing struggle of Alaskans for equality. The other was the refusal of successive Congresses to see and provide for their economic, social, judicial, and political needs. Jackson, in refusing to accept anything less than what he believed was the best for a neglected land and its inhabitants, made many enemies in the territory and in the States. The relative success he achieved in attaining his goals set him apart from others, and his inability or unwillingness to play the role of a politician in the best meaning of the word estranged him further from all groups in Alaska.

There was other background to the Churchill report which involved Jackson personally. Always the memory persisted that he had been jailed once on similar charges. Although his superiors claimed repeatedly that they found not the slightest evidence to support the charges made against him, it was easy to suggest that where there was smoke there was probably fire. It was said too that only Jackson's church affiliation kept him out of jail. True enough, the Church was an influential factor in the life of the territory, and Presidents Harrison and Cleveland were Presbyterians, as were many of their cabinet officers. Under such circumstances, it was not difficult to argue that a guilty Jackson had been shielded from his just fate.

Other denominations vigorously contributed to the effort to raise the moral climate of Alaska, but Jackson kept the Presbyterians in the foreground. Of course he required the help of all groups to combat the evil influences that flourished in a frontier land.

Jackson's seemingly inexhaustible physical reserves showed the effects of years of depletion by 1906—though it was not perceptible to all. His hair was thinner and grayer. His beard was white and sparse. The crease that cut across his forehead to the bridge of his nose was more pronounced than ever. Otherwise, there were few physical signs to indicate that the years had taken any great toll, for he held his head erect and his shoulders straight. He was as convinced as ever of the correctness of his efforts. Perhaps most of all, he was confirmed in his belief that men with vision and faith must be prepared to travel a solitary path.

One event about this time provided him with some comfort. Sir Wilfred Grenfell, the founder of the Deep Sea Fisherman's

Mission in Newfoundland, had been interested in Jackson's reindeer work. Grenfell was satisfied that the project had succeeded and concluded that he could bring reindeer to Newfoundland and achieve similar results.

"I mean to go in for these reindeer," Sir Wilfred wrote to Jackson, "and I am putting up the money myself, as at present I have not been able to move the government. I think shortly, due to your admirable reports, I will be able to do so."

The parallel to his own experience must have made Jackson smile. The two missionaries carried on a brief correspondence about the reindeer, with Jackson offering the kind of advice that Grenfell felt would provide the basis of "redeeming the people" in Newfoundland. Grenfell asked for assistance in securing one thousand animals. From a hospital bed in Philadelphia where he had undergone an operation long overdue, Jackson wrote to Kjelmann, urging his help. Grenfell replied in December 1907 that the first three hundred reindeer had been landed and the project was well under way.

Jackson had resigned from his post as general agent for education in Alaska by then. On June 13, 1907, he noted in a letter to Elmer Ellsworth Brown, the new United States Commissioner for Education, that "I have recently passed my 74th birthday and completed fifty years of strenuous work for the public welfare. With advancing years and failing health, I feel the necessity of withdrawing from public life. . . . I could not have asked for more hearty co-operation or more generous treatment. . . ."

Brown replied that "the establishment of schools over a wide, extended territory, the beginnings of instruction in the ordinary school subjects, taught in the English language, together with the still more important subjects of moral standards and industrial occupation, and particularly the introduction of the reindeer industry and a system of training which centers in that industry—these are achievements of large significance and leave no doubt that your name will long be held in memory by those who are concerned in the uplift of the Alaskan native. . . ."

A few days after Jackson wrote to the Office of Education, he received an official communication from the Presbyterian Board of Home Missions:

". . . a resolution was adopted to discontinue the little appropriation of $500 which the Board has for a number of years been annually making for you in recognition of the service which you have incidentally rendered to the Board in connection with your yearly visits to Alaska. In connection with the fact that you are no longer able to make those visits and render this service, and in view of the apparent inappropriateness of the action of the Board in supplementing the salary of one who is in the employ of the government . . . [and] in view of this additional fact, that our action in this matter has called forth inquiries, not to say criticism in some quarters—the Board has deemed it advisable to take the above-named action."

The letter also contained words of appreciation for his efforts and ended with "these services can never be forgotten by the church which you have represented and served so faithfully—or the nation which has been blessed by your labors."

One is struck by the mixed blessings that the letter indicated. Jackson, who may also have noticed the same incongruity, responded with some asperity, noting that some official recognition of his long service would have been appropriate. He heard in reply to the effect that such action had been taken by the board and spread on its minutes, but that by some oversight the board had neglected to send him a copy of the resolution.

The Jacksons celebrated their fiftieth wedding anniversary in May 1908. In the summer of the same year they took a trip during which Mrs. Jackson became ill and died. Jackson remained as active as his health would permit until in Baltimore late in the winter of 1909 he contracted a cold that sapped his strength. He recovered and went to Winston Salem, North Carolina, to make an address on Alaska. Shortly thereafter, in April, 1909, he was hospitalized in Asheville, North Carolina, for another operation. It was more than he could stand and he died on May 2. He was buried beside his wife in Minaville, New York, where he had spent his youth.

Several years before Jackson's death, the commander of the United States Revenue Cutter *Thetis*, Lieutenant W. H. Cushing, had been admonished by his superior, C. F. Shoemaker, for not having used good judgment in providing accommodations for Jackson during a cruise to Alaska on official business. Shoemaker's letter, coming from a government official who was a relative outsider in the Jackson story, puts rather pithily most of what needs to be said about the man and his work:

"I presume you never knew Dr. Jackson personally, because if you had, I cannot imagine that you could have paid so little attention to him as indicated in his letter. He is one among the few men to whom the Department has accorded great consideration.

"He is an eminent man in his profession, and whatever others may say, one of the most upright, honorable, and valuable men in any branch of public service.

"He has for years been employed upon Alaskan work for the Department of the Interior, and has an established reputation for probity and integrity. I know it is quite the fashion to ridicule and traduce Dr. Jackson, but I do not believe this 'fashion' is indulged by any decent man who knows him, and

I am certain in saying that however scandalous the talk, and it is nothing but talk, he is in every regard a superior man.

"He has been a cabin passenger in the *Bear* every year for many years, and I have yet to hear that he has ever, in any way, abused any privilege or in any manner made himself obnoxious . . . I am sorry that you did not welcome him to your ship, give him a seat at your table, and treat him like the gentleman he is. . . .

"Surely you could out of the abundant facilities at your disposal, have accorded him comfortable berth in the cabin and made his stay what it should have been made, without the least inconvenience to yourself.

"You may not be aware of the fact, but it is true that Dr. Jackson was very able and largely instrumental in getting through the appropriation for the *Thetis*. His standing here among legislators is of the highest . . ."

A large part of Jackson's significance lies in the attitude with which he responded to the demands made upon him and in his willingness to seek out problems instead of waiting for them to come to him. No need was ever so small, no urgency ever so pressing, no obstacle ever so overwhelming that he was not prepared to meet it directly. Living, in Jackson's code, consisted in making progress. Righteousness to him meant putting things in their proper place, not just talking about it.

It is true that he often involved the Church, sometimes against its will and often to the point of exasperation, in facing responsibilities—not so much because it would not act, but because he believed there could be no excuse for delay. In his pioneer missionary work west of the Mississippi River he comprehended the obligation of the Church to establish a spiritual climate in which sound social and economic progress could take place. In Alaska he recognized the fact that the Church had to take substantial measures to improve social and economic conditions even if it had to act alone.

His life was a good example of what the citizen-clergyman should be: neither the one before the other, but the two blending in common purpose, doing all to the glory of God. His life was clear evidence that a minister involved in social welfare work is not and cannot expect to be immune from criticism but must accept it as part of the price to be paid for saving bodies and souls.

Although it is true that a relatively loose organizational structure permitted him to work in freewheeling fashion, it also imposed a pattern of action upon him, for if he had waited for official approval of his projects, many of them would not have been begun. He combined the drive of the doer with the talents of the planner. Jackson was tactician as well as strategist.

He was never averse to linking spiritual concerns with the processes of the secular world on behalf of those interests in which he saw the Church and the State involved in a cause important to the welfare of each. He lobbied, encouraged others to lobby, and offered advice to church people on how to influence Congress. The claim that he was interfering with political and social processes in Alaska never bothered him. He understood that the Church could not meet problems of rehabilitation alone and that the State had a moral responsibility to share them. At the same time, it was inconceivable to him that the Church should slacken its efforts when the community began to assume a larger role in raising its own levels. He wanted the Church involved in such effort if for no other reason than that it could be effective in raising standards.

Jackson played another role in the development of Church life in the nineteenth century far more important than is generally realized. During his early career when his efforts were hampered by lack of funds, he and others became convinced that there was a need for a central women's organization to support home missionary work among the Indians and Spanish-speaking people in the Southwest. He organized the *Rocky Mountain Presbyterian* in part for the purpose of stimulating women's interest in missions. With the approval of Henry Kendall, Jackson carried on a writing and speaking campaign to effect organized assistance among women of the church. Small missionary groups were already aiding individual church school projects in Arizona and New Mexico, and a women's organization of limited scope was performing important services on behalf of home and foreign missions, but they were not suitable for the massive approach which Jackson visualized. Repeated efforts to develop a woman's arm of the Church on a national scale for the sole benefit of home missions had met with repeated opposition. Some felt it would detract from support for the foreign board. Others had doubts about the wisdom of spending money to aid the Indians and Spanish-speaking people. Finally, with the backing of Kendall, Jackson received approval to encourage the formation of a woman's organization to provide financial support for the home board. The denomination itself approved the plan in 1874. Four years later, still not satisfied with progress, Jackson acted on his own in urging a group of women to meet in a kind of rump missionary body in New York, sending out invitations to the meeting over his own name. This act hastened the formation of the Women's Executive Committee of Home Missions of the Presbyterian Church.

It is very clear from the record that Jackson could not have done his work as effectively as he did without the aid of certain leading women of the church. A good portion of his success in the Rocky Mountains and in Alaska resulted from his ability to get the women behind his plans.

As circumstances required, he worked at being a pastor, missionary and evangelist, educator, editor, reporter, empire builder, government official, historian, pamphleteer, lobbyist, fund raiser, reformer, explorer, colporteur, tour manager, diplomat, political strategist, and philanthropist. The distance he traveled in fulfilling these roles does not measure the extent of his impact, even though it can be estimated roughly at about one million miles.

He played a tremendous part in the opening of the Rocky Mountain area to the Church. No history of the interrelationship of Church and State in the land west of the Mississippi can be complete without taking into account his superlative field generalship, although Alaska is where one finds a more direct result of his efforts. Today, one hundred and twenty-five ministers, teachers, parish workers, and children's leaders carry on the Presbyterian work he began in Alaska. Thirty-three Presbyterian churches have a membership of about five thousand, although the majority of them are as yet not self-sustaining. Three of the congregations are Eskimo; the one at Point Barrow having a membership of five hundred and sixty.

Although Jackson was limited in means of travel present-day Presbyterian work in Alaska uses every available facility. The mobile ministry of the Board of National Missions covers hundreds of miles of the Alaskan Highway and its branches, reaching construction camps, trailer parks—wherever there are families. What is perhaps the world's longest "church" stretches along part of the route of the Alaska Railroad, serving railroad families and men working at isolated mines or stationed at missile sites. The Presbyterian "navy" consists of two motor ships—the *Princeton Hall* and the *Anna Jackman,* the latter named for the wife of Dr. J. Earl Jackman who now directs Presbyterian work in Alaska. They ply the waters of southeast Alaska, bringing pastoral care to isolated settlements, fishing centers, logging camps, and weather stations. The minister at Barrow flies a single-engine plane—the one now in use is *Arctic Messenger III*—to scattered villages above the Arctic Circle. The Presbyterians also co-operate in ministering to those who man the nation's distant early warning system and other units of the armed forces. Radio station KSEW at Sitka is owned and operated by the church.

In terms of numbers, Presbyterian work in Alaska today is small when compared to the scores of churches in the Western States which witness to Jackson's efforts. But in terms of the difficulties he encountered in Alaska, and the magnitude of the task faced by those who followed him there, the Church in the forty-ninth state stands as the finest monument to Jackson's efforts.

In the field of higher education, Sheldon Jackson Junior College, related to the United Presbyterian Church in the U.S.A., is an outgrowth of the Sitka industrial training school. The school had an enrollment of one hundred and sixty-five students in 1959, most of whom were in the high school department. The students are mainly Indians, Eskimos, Aleuts, and mixed bloods. There are about forty-three white students, half of whom are on the junior college level. The president of the school, R. Rolland Armstrong, was very active in getting statehood for Alaska.

The Sheldon Jackson Museum, located on the junior college campus and now operated by the school, is another of Jackson's important contributions to Alaska. Its contents are described as "a fine collection of Russian material reminiscent of their tenure, as well as a remarkable collection of aboriginal artifacts," which Jackson gathered from far and wide in Alaska. He donated the frame building that first housed the museum when it opened in 1890. Then, better to preserve the collection, he paid for the construction of the present octagonal concrete building which was completed in 1896.

Alaska's 586,400 square miles had an estimated population of 191,000 on July 1, 1958—between 60,000 and 70,000 being military personnel and dependents. Eskimos, Indians, and Aleuts number thirty-four thousand, an increase of about five thousand since 1900. The white population has increased about five times since then. In terms of its ability to produce wealth, which Jackson always insisted was an important factor in stepping up aid to the territory, Alaska is only starting to give proof that the optimistic claims made on its behalf were never exaggerated. The total volume of Alaskan business in 1957 was around five hundred and sixty-six million dollars, involving three hundred and thirteen companies. Retail sales amounted to two hundred and seven million dollars. The output of the fishing industries was seventy-nine million; mining and timber were twenty-nine million each; farming and furs were each four million. One of Alaska's two burgeoning industries is the paper pulp business. The other is oil. Major oil companies have commitments of over one hundred million dollars for future development in Alaska. Some experts believe that Alaska's hydroelectric power potential is the greatest in the world.

Considering Alaska's actual and potential values, one can have only the highest admiration for those who struggled unceasingly to prove Alaska's worth to the nation. Jackson stands high in their ranks.

Much credit is due Jackson for his persistence in keeping Alaska's needs before the nation at a time when the country was preoccupied with social, economic, and political problems that were closer at hand. He was tenacious in his opinions about Alaska's educational requirements and how best they could be met. He was equally determined to help Alaska's native population and constant in defense of the means by which he sought to improve their situation when others in and outside of Alaska would have ignored the problem. Above all, he believed that nothing less than adherence to the highest moral standards should be required of public officials and he never expected less of himself.

Granted that Jackson rubbed some people the wrong way, one cannot deny the accuracy of his vision about Alaska's future or ignore the amazing amount of physical and spiritual energy he expended to achieve his objectives. He spent himself without stint to spread God's kingdom upon earth. It is indeed fortunate that Jackson, one of the last great frontier missionaries of the Church, accepted the call to labor on the last American frontier—Alaska—with a devotion and courage equaled by few.

INDEX